Travellers' Italy

a guide to eight routes throughout Italy

Arthur Eperon is one of the most experienced and best known travel writers in Europe. Since leaving the RAF in 1945 he has worked as a journalist in various capacities often involving travel. He has concentrated on travel writing for the past ten years and contributed to many publications including *The Times, Daily Telegraph, Sun, Woman's Own, Popular Motoring* and the *TV Times*. He has appeared on radio and television and for five years was closely involved in Thames Television's programme *Wish you were here*. His intimate and extensive knowledge of France and its food and wine resulted in the 1979 Pan book *Travellers' France*, featured in the BBC *Holiday 80* programme.

Travellers'

a guide to eight major routes throughout Italy

Arthur Eperon

ITALy

Introduction by Frank Bough
Maps and drawings by Ken Smith

Pan Original
Pan Books and the British Broadcasting Corporation

Also by Arthur Eperon
in Pan Books/BBC
Travellers' France

First published 1980 by Pan Books Ltd,
Cavaye Place, London SW10 9PG
and the British Broadcasting Corporation,
35 Marylebone High Street, London W1M 4AA
© Arthur Eperon 1980
Introduction © Frank Bough 1980
Maps and drawings by Ken Smith
ISBN 0 330 26302 1 (Pan)
ISBN 0 563 17913 9 (BBC)
Printed in England by Chorley & Pickersgill Ltd, Leeds

Acknowledgements

My sincere thanks to all the Italian and British friends who have helped me to discover and enjoy Italy over thirty years, including John Greenwood, formerly of the Royal Opera House, Covent Garden, and the Italian State Tourist Office in London, who first taught me to love Italy; my many friends at CIT, the Italian tour-operating company in England; British Airways, who have done much to help me make final checks on all my fly-drive routes; my wife, travel writer Barbara Clegg, who discovered many of these nice places on my routes; my old friends Fernando Savarese of Le Axidie Hotel, near Vico Equense, and Janek Pagani, who now runs the Napoleon Hotel in Rome – two Italian anglophiles, whose helpful advice I have treasured over years; Catherine Bruzzone, who kindly corrected my appalling Italian spelling, and Jeffrey Rayner, who first explored Calabria with me when the roads were better fitted for mules than motors.

Arthur Eperon

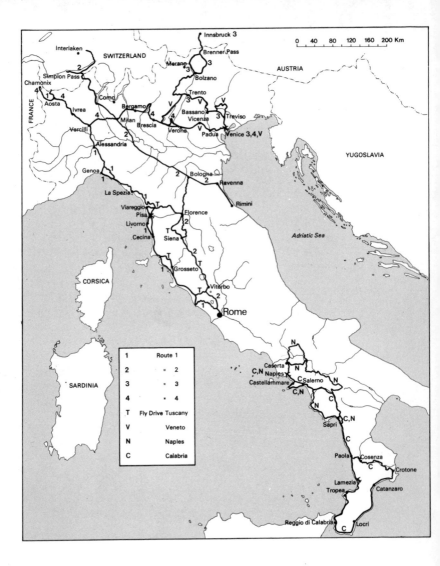

Contents

Introduction
by Frank Bough

Last year when BBC Television's *Holiday 80*
programme asked my wife, Nesta, and me to road-test
Arthur Eperon's *Travellers' France*, we could never
have imagined what a desperate need both
programme and book revealed. Chris Sadler's
delightful camerawork, under the direction of Clem
Vallance, showed a tantalizing flash of the petticoats
of La Belle France that, astonishingly, British
holidaymakers never knew existed. Seven short
programmes, not one of which reached five minutes in
length, on the delights of rambling gently by car
through the rural interior of a country that's our
closest continental neighbour, separated from us by
only a few miles of English Channel! What we know
for certain is that over three hundred thousand people
leapt from their winter fireplaces and bought Arthur's
book. In how many of them the spirit of Marco Polo
survived until the summer we'll never know. But in
1980, several lazy little French auberges and many
Logis de France had never seen the like of it before, as
bookings for accommodation poured in, followed by
fleets of GB plates, all eager to admire the countryside
and wash down the patrons' coq au vin with even
more vin!

Nesta and I were among them, because we went
back. We decided to follow a different route, but one
also recommended by Mr Eperon. At first we avoided
staying at any of the places he enthused about, fearing
hordes of Britishers, waving *Travellers' France* under
our noses, and holding us personally responsible for
the quality of the cuisine! However, his description of
the Relais Fleurie at a little place called Pouilly with
gardens running down to the Loire, and of the fresh
salmon à l'orange, was too much. I sat outside in the

car, turned my collar up, and sent Nesta inside to make the arrangements. We stayed, and the place was enchanting; those of my fellow countrymen who were there too were far too busy tucking into their salmon to bother us!

Well, there had to be a sequel. This is it: *Travellers' Italy*, another Eperon classic which we've also had the opportunity of trying out for the *Holiday* programme. There are eight routes. You can drive all the way if you want to and have the time, or as a variation, if you're impatient to get to Italy quickly, there are several suggested fly-drive schemes. Nesta and I flew to Pisa, and then combined two of Arthur's routes, one in the Tuscany area and the other centred on Venice.

Tuscany was a delight, like a children's painting. At the time we were there, in late June, the wild flowers along the roadside and in the fields were sensational – in such profusion as we'd never seen before – and the colours were quite brilliant.

Neither of us had ever been to Venice, and when I tell you that Robin Swain, the sound recordist in our BBC camera crew and a hard-bitten international traveller to boot, told us that Venice was his favourite European city, and that he couldn't wait to get back, you'll know that it is a unique experience.

There were places we wanted to keep to ourselves, like San Gimignano, the Village of Towers, and Castiglione della Pescaia, a jewel of a seaside resort on the west coast, north of Rome.

We discovered Verona, certainly our favourite town; and that Italian wine is not just plonk, but can be superb, and that pasta is not just pasta either, but infinite in its variety, and it's the local trattoria down the back street that makes it best.

It seems to us that many countries are far cheaper than Britain for food and accommodation, and that's certainly true of Italy, which won't murder your wallet unduly. So *Travellers' Italy* suggests one or two places where you can spoil yourself a little if the funds are lasting out well.

You'll find one very significant difference between Italy and France. In France, the village or roadside restaurant is traditional to the whole country, but in Italy the villagers eat mostly at home. It's in the town you'll find the hostelries and the eating and watering holes, and it's in the towns too that you can enjoy the sight of a country that's magnificently blessed with a sense of history, with the most wonderful buildings, villas and palaces.

The Eperon philosophy remains the same. You're not really going anywhere at all. You're travelling in Italy. So try the routes he suggests by all means, but be adventurous. Turn off the highway, go over the hill, and you'll end up beating Arthur Eperon at his own game!

Frank and Nesta Bough

Preface

A respected motoring correspondent reminded me that you can now drive off the ferry at Dunkirk and go all the way to the 'toe' of Italy without leaving a motorway.

Yes, you can.

If you felt adventurous, you might allow yourself the luxury of a couple of hours in Paris to see the Louvre, a glance at Milan Cathedral, a flip round Florence, and a drive through Rome from St Peter's to the Colosseum before catching the ferry to Sicily.

But if your business is that urgent, why not fly?

I am not sneering at the magnificent Autostrada del Sole, the motorway running through the heart of Italy to the toe. It is a superb engineering achievement, useful not only to industry and to the economic future of Italy's south but also to explorers seeking the remoter hideaways of central and southern Italy. However, to discover Italy's treasures, you must get off it.

And it is surely a good time to rediscover Italy now that the exchange rate for the £ is in our favour and Spanish prices have risen.

For centuries knowledgeable travellers like the writers Byron, Shelley, Goethe and Montaigne or, in more recent times, H. V. Morton and Jan Morris have regarded Italy as the most rewarding country to explore in Europe – more so even than France or Greece.

Most of us have tended to think of it, as we have of
Spain, as a place for seaside package tours to sunny
beaches, of which Italy has plenty, and for the odd
short trip to Venice, Rome and perhaps Florence. But
tourist figures show that more of us are tiring of
simply beach-lounging, and there is no doubt that TV
programmes have helped to stimulate our interest in
how people lived in the past, in the lovely things they
produced and, not least, in beautiful scenery.

By discovering Italy, I do not mean simply the great
old cities, but the lesser-known towns and villages,
the mountains, the lakes which are one of Italy's
special joys, and more remote, little-known areas like
the hills along the spine of Italy and the deep south.

It is easy to think of Italy as just a big open-air
museum of Greek, Roman, medieval and
Renaissance art and architecture – beautiful, but a
little too highbrow for us.

It is not. It is one of the liveliest countries in the world,
full of action, sometimes too noisy, nearly always
fun. The first surprise is the number of happy and
smiling faces you see in a country rumoured often to
be on the brink of economic disaster.

There is much to do and see besides admiring the
old. Our routes take you to beaches or lakes, through
some of the finest mountain scenery in Europe, to
splendid areas for food and wine – with even a
chance to turn racing driver for one lap of the Monza
Grand Prix track if you and your car feel up to it. You
will also see a lot of handsome people. On the whole,
Italians are better looking than the British, and
although you will not see a Sophia Loren on every
street, you will see a lot of girls running her quite
close. A tip for young bachelors: Italian girls may be
very liberated in their behaviour these days but they
like old-fashioned manners. Even that girl smiling at
you as if she has just rolled out of bed and would not
mind being rolled back in again expects the
sophisticated, old-style approach. And Italian men
are experts at giving it.

In Italy the old comes to life. As I have found over thirty years, you have only to wander round cities like Siena and Vicenza, Verona and Pisa to relive their fascinating stories by looking at the buildings in which people lived, worked and prayed and at the beautiful things they made not just for decoration but to use every day.

Italy repays a little homework before you go – the reading of a few books about the places you mean to see. You will find in them stories of hatred, love, intrigue, glory and violence which make the most spectacular TV fiction seem a little pale. And, if like most people on this earth you cannot tell Romanesque architecture from Gothic and are a bit hazy about art styles, you will find a fair, quick summary in the front of the green *Michelin Guide* to Italy.

Italian people tend to be volatile, passionate and friendly. I can happily just sit outside a café and watch them going about their daily business. Most are fiercely proud, and although many must live by their wits or go under, they are not the grasping, swindling people that unknowledgeable critics would have us believe.

They will love you if you are *simpatico* – an almost untranslatable word meaning roughly that you are friendly, genial, not condescending, understanding and preferably soft-spoken.

In one of my favourite holiday hotels in Italy a British judge got a reputation for extreme meanness and, true to himself, left without tipping anyone. But the headwaiter liked him, for he was a 'gentleman' – always polite and smiling to the staff, never raised his voice, snapped his fingers or became impatient. He was *simpatico*. It will get you nowhere to shout at anyone in Italy. They can shout back louder and faster.

As in Provence and many Greek isles, the light is the essence of the countryside. The light is golden; it

intensifies colours and clarifies outlines. Nothing is blurred – the blue sea, the yellow or volcanic-grey beaches, the lakes and mountains, the brown and red stone and brickwork of the churches and villas, the white marble of buildings in Tuscany, the baroque fountains which can turn a simple village square into a place of serene magic.

I heard an American complaining that Italy was falling apart. 'It's like a '55 Ford in a breakers' yard,' he said. To me it is like a slightly neglected, travel-worn Rover which still runs sweetly, looks noble and interesting and would gladden the heart of any enthusiast. Italy has so many magnificent old buildings; it simply cannot keep them all in perfect repair.

The trick when visiting cities is to park and walk, not only to see more but to stay relaxed. Streets tend to be narrow and very crowded with traffic; casual parking-places are rare, and drivers get impatient. The Italian becomes a different man behind the wheel of a car. He has not forgotten that Tazio Nuvolari and Ascari were two of the greatest racing drivers in history, and thinks he is one of them. He never waits, even if it means mounting a pavement to get by. Happily, once out of town, the roads are usually fairly clear because any Italian thinks that you are slightly mad to use any other road if there is any chance of getting somewhere by motorway – despite motorway tolls in all but the far south.

A few years back, when Italy finally brought out a highway code, one rule said that motorists must give way to trains at level crossings. I showed it to my friend Tom Wisdom, the journalist who had recently beaten the Italians to win the touring class of the Mille Miglia, the 1,000-mile round-Italy race.

'I bet they don't, you know,' he said.

They have become a little less aggressive since then, thanks to roadside fines, but it is a matter of pride for Italians to overtake foreign drivers. Let them. You are on holiday. Let them go. If you make a mistake, apologize with gestures.

Most of the routes in this book are north of Rome, and drivers tend to be less volatile in Tuscany, Piedmont and Veneto than around Naples.

I have offered a choice of two routes to Rome (one with a choice of making for the Adriatic resorts from Bologna), and two to Venice. They avoid the motorways most of the time. But if you want to spend longer in Florence, perhaps, or Verona, and you are a bit pressed for time, you can take to the motorway for a while.

I have also included four 'fly-drive' routes because I believe that Italy is excellent fly-drive country. You fly to the area you choose, then hire a car. If you drive all the way, you either cross France on motorways, which is no fun and still uses four days of your precious freedom getting to Italy and back, or you dawdle across France and enjoy it. Then you have little time to explore Italy – and might not even reach it. The ideal is both to dawdle across France *and* explore Italy but, alas, few of us have time and money together for that sort of trip.

Fortunately there are some good fly-drive offers these days which cut the cost of car hire. British Airways, for instance, have tied up with Avis car hire to offer cut-price tours, flying to several cities. So have CIT, the Italian state-owned operator with a complete British operation (CIT, 262 High Street, Croydon CR9 1LL). Check with both when you have decided where you want to go. Some magazines have suggested that you can save money by getting a cheap air fare, then hiring a car from a local cut-price firm in Italy. The cheap air fare is all right if you are not tied by business or family to an exact return date. Cheap air fares are to fill seats unfilled at the last moment. Whatever anyone tells you, I can assure you that you may have to wait to get home. During the last year I have met dozens of Britons at airports, including Italian airports, who bought cheap tickets and were desperately waiting for a plane back days after their expected return date. As for cut-price car hire, that may be fine if you have perfect Italian and a legal mind. Can you really read the small print in the contract? One of my readers thought he had bought total cover. He was hit by a tearaway driver and found himself liable for the first £500 of damage under a small-print clause. He was not the only one, either. It just is not worth the risk to save a few pounds.

I recommend fly-drive particularly for southern Italy, especially Calabria, an area of enormous interest but little known to Britons except for a few coastal resorts.

The most popular routes into Italy for people driving
from Britain are the Mont Blanc tunnel and the
motorway along the French Riviera. The ordinary
Riviera coast road still has frontier queues in
midsummer, though nothing like the two- and
three-hour queues motorists knew before the
motorway was completed. It is possible to join each
of our routes from some of the other crossings into
Italy, although obviously it would be silly, for
instance, to use the Riviera crossing on your way to
Venice, or the Brenner Pass on your way to Pisa.

Italian roads are eccentrically variable. Occasionally
a road which is marked in red on the map, and
therefore important and presumably better than a
green road, may be pot-holed and twisting, while the
green road can be in fine condition. I have mentioned
some red roads to avoid on my routes.

In the south, mountain roads can be quite hard work
for the driver because they twist, rise and fall, so you
cannot keep up high average speeds. The average
can drop to twenty m.p.h. But please don't let me
frighten you. Any reasonably experienced driver can

handle them. Just give yourself the odd rest to admire the scenery and don't be too optimistic about how far you will travel in a day.

Maps cannot show all the twists and turns of mountain roads, so it is important to read distances carefully on them. That road cutting across the mountains may be as long, and may certainly take longer to drive, than the 'long way round'.

The Michelin map of Italy No. 988, or a similar Italian map, is essential for all routes but does not include the names of all the places I have mentioned. Useful for all routes, and almost essential for fly-drive routes, are the area road maps. Those I use are published by Litografia Artistica Cartografica, in Florence (Firenze in Italian), and can be bought for just over £1 in Italy. One place in Britain which stocks them, although it may run out of the odd one, is Geographia, 63 Fleet Street, London EC4. The ones you want are the *carte regionali* (regional maps) of, for instance, Toscana (Tuscany) or Tre Venezie (the whole Veneto area and around it) or Calabria.

Italian road regulations are much the same as in the rest of Europe. However, you are expected to carry a translation of your driving licence, which you can get from the AA, RAC or the Italian State Tourist Office, 201 Regent Street, London W1.

Seat belts are compulsory, and the Italian police are often tougher about this than about speeding; they are also stricter than in Britain on drinking and driving, and you can get six months in prison. Speed limits are 50 k.p.h. (31 m.p.h.) in all built-up areas, 80-110 k.p.h. (50-68 m.p.h.) on normal roads, 90-140 k.p.h. (60-87 m.p.h.) on motorways, according to the size of your engine. If you have a small hire car, which is not allowed to travel over 80 or 90 k.p.h., there should be a disc on its tail giving this figure. Police traps are less frequent than in France, but fines are heavier. Fines of £400 have been enforced on occasion for breach of speed limits. Dipped headlights are compulsory in tunnels, even well-lit ones, and there are plenty of tunnels. You can get away legally with your own insurance policy, or the old Green Card, but these give you only the legal minimum third-party insurance. You may not be covered against theft, damage, or injury to passengers. Then there are such problems as getting help if the car breaks down, or if a member of the party gets ill or injured, and such unexpected items as freighting spares from Britain, a hire car to continue a journey, hotel costs while awaiting repairs.

So do take out a full insurance. The nearest thing to a comprehensive insurance is offered by the AA, the RAC or specialist brokers like Europ Assistance and Perry.

In EEC countries such as Italy you are entitled to the same medical treatment as insured nationals of the country. But do get form E111 before you go; this may save you paying certain medical costs on the spot, then waiting to recover the money when you get home (you need booklet SA28 from your local social security office to tell you how to apply for this form).

Food and beds

Walking around Italian city streets these days, you could think that people lived on pizza and ice cream. Eating in Britain's 'Italian' restaurants you could believe that Italian cooking was anything covered in oily tomato sauce with garlic and topped with cheese.

Truth is that Italian cooking is probably second only to French in Europe. Pastas like spaghetti, ravioli, tagliatelle and tortellini freshly made in the restaurant and freshly cooked are a different dish from those we make from pasta in cardboard boxes or those from the freezer or can. Hams are superb, especially cured or smoked and eaten raw; fish is usually fresh and grilled over charcoal, excellent even if you cannot recognize or name it. Beef may not be very good outside Tuscany, lamb is very dear, but veal and chicken, from free-range farms, and pork are succulent and superbly cooked in hundreds of ways.

Cooking is regional, so almost the same dish may have a different name in different places, or the same name may be used for different dishes. This makes menus a little hard to follow.

If the waiter speaks any English at all, and most do, it is best to go through the menu with him, or you could end up living on ham, spaghetti and veal cutlets, which would be dull and un-Italian. Rather than do that, look around at what Italians are eating and point to it, or just pick a dish at random and risk it. You will probably be pleasantly surprised.

An example of the waywardness of menus is prodetto. In Tuscany it is a soup of stock, bread and beaten eggs; at Adriatic resorts like Rimini it is a fish stew, which is called cacciucco in Tuscany and often made with red wine; in Venice it is called broeto. The pasta mostly called tagliatelle is called fettuccine around Rome. The delicious cushion pasta, ravioli, comes with various fillings from meat to cheese and spinach or fish. There are many local names for pasta, especially in Calabria. Be prepared, too, for pasta in brodo – that is, soup with pasta floating in it.

Fritto misto to me once meant pieces of shellfish and fish fried in batter. Other versions use all vegetables, or meat and vegetables.

Look first on the menu for antipasto (roughly, hors d'oeuvre), especially around Bologna, Parma, Modena and the Veneto, for it includes the raw hams which are splendid, sausages such as salame and mortadella sausage which is fresh and delightful, not the tasteless rubber we get after it has been frozen in Britain. Many Italians prefer the prosciutto crudo (raw cured ham) of San Daniele to the famous Parma ham, and I like the rougher country and mountain versions – less subtle, stronger, chewier – or Parma's capocollo (cured shoulder of pork).

To add to the subtlety of Italian menus, proud restaurant owners call dishes after themselves or after their mothers; mother is queen of the family house and kitchen in Italy.

Italians like a bit of pomp and show when they eat out and will pay extra for décor, waiters in white coats and attentive headwaiters. This could cost you L15,000-20,000 (around £7.50-10) for a three-course meal, but it will probably be very good and cheaper than in a similar restaurant at home. I tend to think that you are usually better off at a less-showy place where men or girls or even the *padrone* in short sleeves will serve you while mum or the *padrone* does the cooking. This is the nearest thing to a French bistro; the food will probably be just as good, even if the choice is smaller, and the price L8,000-12,000 (about £4-6). The house wine will cost about £1 or under, a better wine £1.50-2.

If you want a light lunch, such as pasta for under £1 or a main course for under £2, these places will serve it, but they will make it plain that you will starve on such meagre rations. Lunch is the main meal in Italy, and four courses are fairly normal.

The pizzeria is becoming more popular and most serve many other dishes and even full meals as well as pizza. Pizzas are cooked in an open oven, often over wood, are absolutely freshly made, and superb. They bear no relation to the factory-made, freezer-kept 'pizza pie' in Britain. In some pizzerias, there is a take-away service; and students buy just a slice of pizza for their lunch, for about 25p.

Some restaurants, mostly in towns or resorts, serve set-price tourist menus at around £3-4 including cover charge, local tax and service, but these are often uninspired, and you can get a better meal by choosing cheaper dishes off the *carta*, the list of dishes.

The Italians do not go in for set menus in the same way as the French; you choose from the *carta* and each dish has its price marked, so that, for instance, spaghetti might be cheaper than ravioli. All restaurants have a charge for 'cover and bread', varying from L400 in the cheaper trattoria to L600 in a medium restaurant and up to L1,000 in a first-class restaurant. Service is usually added – ten or fifteen per cent. But in bigger restaurants and in towns you are expected to tip the waiter – usually another ten per cent.

Italy has fewer country restaurants or little hotels than France. Even Italian farmworkers often go home to the nearest small town after work. And these days there are fewer little family-run hotels offering meals. With food prices rising, they cannot compete with restaurants with a bigger turnover of eaters, and they are cutting losses and reducing staff by offering only bed and breakfast.

There is a shortage of medium-priced hotels in Italy. The *luxe* hotels are some of the best in the world and appropriately dear. First-class hotels are usually very good, cheaper than in Britain, but more than most travellers want to pay on a tour. Simple hotels and

alberghi, usually very clean, with basic facilities like toilet and shower to most rooms, have not the same atmosphere as a Logis de France. Rooms tend to be small, especially bathrooms. At *my* width, I have actually had to back out of them! Prices are a little higher than in France and value not quite so good, but lower prices than in Britain.

You can always look at a room before booking it. Ask its full price, including local taxes and service, because some hotels include these, while others add them when you pay your bill. Behind the bedroom door, or more sneakily behind the wardrobe door, you should find the official price of your room, with tax and service shown too. You should not have to pay more.

Single rooms are rare, but not so rare as in France. Some have a washbasin but no toilet or shower.

Except with individualistic hotels with attractive meals to offer, it pays to go out to a restaurant to eat.

Important: The prices quoted in this book for meals are for an average three-course meal without wine. Prices vary according to which dishes you choose. Hotel prices are mostly for a double room without breakfast, although some lower prices are for single rooms.

The prices are correct as far as possible up to autumn 1980. But inflation in Italy is currently running at about as high a level as in Britain, and prices rose about fifteen per cent between summer 1979 and summer 1980.

So it is quite possible that, by summer 1981, you may have to add fifteen per cent or so to the prices quoted, to account for inflation.

Security

In all tourist resorts these days, including London, it is asking for trouble to leave parcels and especially suitcases on view in a parked car. If you must leave them at all, hide them in the boot. Similarly, it is dangerous to carry money, passport or credit cards in a back pocket or any pocket not firmly buttoned down, or to carry these things in a handbag which can be easily opened. Professional pickpockets act like lightning.

It is particularly foolish to do these things in Italy. I do not think there are significantly more thieves in Italy – they are just more efficient! The worst cities for pickpockets, handbag snatchers and car thieves are Naples, Turin, Venice and Rome. Many Italian drivers now have car radios which are easily removed, and they take them into hotels and restaurants with them to avoid car break-ins.

Main tunnels and passes into Italy

Riviera road: A8 (France) to A10 (Italy) motorway above Menton-Ventimiglia or A7 S1 coast road Menton-Ventimiglia.

Road tunnels
Great St Bernard: south of Martigny (Switzerland) to north of Aosta (Italy); 1,830 m (6,000 ft) above sea level; 6 km long; wheel chains may be needed to approach it in winter; tolls (1980) for cars 12-27 Swiss francs.

Mont Blanc: Chamonix (France) to Courmayeur (Italy); 11 km long; wheel chains needed very occasionally mid-winter; cars 35-75 French francs.

Fréjus: Modane (France) to Bardonecchia (Italy); 12.7 km long; opening delayed because approach road from Italian side not finished; should be open by July 1981; alternative train car-carrier tunnel.

Rail car-carrier tunnels
Simplon: Brig (Switzerland) to Iselle (Italy) open all the year; frequent service; no booking necessary; time about 20 minutes.

Mont Cénis (Fréjus): Modane (France) to Bardonecchia (Italy); 13.7 km long; services have been unreliable during building of parallel road tunnel, and occasionally it has been closed, but should be operating effectively by spring 1981; cars 30-42 French francs.

Main passes

Brenner: Innsbruck (Austria) to Vipiteno (Italy); usually open; motorway or main road.

Great St Bernard: Martigny (Switzerland) to Aosta (Italy); usually closed late October to early June (alternative road tunnel); good surface but narrow – maximum width for vehicles (8¼ ft).

Larch (Maddalena): Barcelonnette (France) to Cuneo (Italy); very light traffic; narrow and rough in places, nice scenery; reaches Italy on S20, 85 km south of Turin; closed November to May.

Mont Cénis: Lanslebourg (France) to Susa (Italy); easy driving but surface poor in places; usually closed November to May.

Montgenèvre: Briançon (France) to Sestriere (Italy); from west of Grenoble, road on Italian side leads to Turin, where there are motorways to Milan or to Alessandria (Route 1); easy modern road, usually open.

Resia: Pfunds (Austria) to Malles (Italy); usually open; alternative to Brenner.

Simplon: Brig (Switzerland) to Domodossola (Italy); rebuilt road makes it an easy drive but 21 km long and maximum width for cars 2.5 m (8¼ ft); closed occasionally November to April; rail alternative.

Splügen: Switzerland to Italy; *not recommended*; narrow, winding, hairpin bends; badly guarded edges; dodgy tunnels and galleries; road narrows in places to 3 m (10 ft); cars over 2.3 m (7½ ft) wide not allowed. Usually closed October to early June.

How to use this book

Each page is divided into three columns.

The left-hand column gives you the road numbers to follow along the route, the places you will go through and towns or villages which are worth stopping at. The distances are given in parentheses.

The middle column recommends places to eat and stay at.

The right-hand column mentions points of historic, architectural or scenic interest about the area.

Route 1
Mont Blanc tunnel/
Great St Bernard
to Rome
(via Pisa)

This is the road to Rome for people who enjoy medieval cities, Renaissance treasures and history, but also want their share of beautiful scenery and bathing beaches.

It begins with some of the finest mountain scenery in Europe, drops down to the Tuscany coast, where you can choose between resting and bathing at lively resorts like Viareggio or turn a short way off the road to one of the small beach resorts south of Pisa such as Donorattico.

You miss the glories of Florence and Siena, but you see old and more intimate cities like the remarkable walled city of Lucca, Pisa, and the Etruscan city of Tarquinia. You could see Florence and Siena by following Route 2 on the way home.

If you are taking the Riviera route to Italy, join at Genoa. But then you will miss those magnificent mountains.

A splendid route for eating and drinking. The Aosta valley leans heavily towards French cuisine, uses butter rather than oil, mountain dairy products, game and trout. Fonduta, made from local fontina cheese, is more subtle than Swiss fondue.

Further down the route, in Piedmont, butter and cream still reign; rice is used more than pasta, especially in risottos, like risotto alla Valdestana – rice with parmesan and fontina cheeses mixed to make a thick cream. Try here bagna cauda – a 'hot bath' of butter, oil, garlic and anchovies into which you dip raw vegetables – and bollito – a mixture of beef, chicken, sausage and pigs' trotters, boiled and served with salsa verde (a very piquant green sauce of parsley, onion, basil, marjoram, capers, anchovy and hard-boiled egg mixed with oil and lemon juice); also try gnocchi alla fontina (semolina pasta cooked in milk, rolled in cheese and breadcrumbs, then fried – delicious and filling). The white truffle of Piedmont, claimed to be the world's greatest fungus, is glorious and very expensive.

Around Alessandria, you pass near to wine country producing not only the refreshing bubbly Asti Spumante but the great Barolo, a strong, highly flavoured red wine of Châteauneuf-du-Pape standards; Barbaresco, similar but drier and less flavoured; Barbera, dark, acidic and excellent with rich food, and Grignolino, light and red, suitable for lunch.

Tuscany is one of the great areas in the world for cuisine. Cooking is fairly simple, because they produce beef, chickens and fish good enough to be simply charcoal-grilled. Bistecca alla Fiorentina, local T-bone steak, is reckoned by Italians to be the best steak in Europe. Baccalà, salt cod, is better than it sounds, so are fagioli (white beans) the various ways they are cooked here. Burrida is fish soup, cacciucco a fish soup made with red wine and spices. The raw ham (prosciutto crudo, as opposed to cotto – cooked) is excellent. Spaghetti con le telline is thin spaghetti with cockles, garlic, parsley, tomato, small hot peppers and oil. Zuppa di datteri alla Viareggina is made from 'sea dates' – tiny shellfish – with tomatoes and garlic.

Red Chianti wine is Tuscan, of course, but Tuscany also produces some fair dry white wines with some body.

Later we are in the Roman province of Latium, where they call tagliatelle pasta 'fettuccine'. You find good macaroni dishes, the famous trippa alla Romana (tripe in tomato and meat sauce flavoured with mint and topped with grated pecorino cheese). Spaghetti alla carbonara, favoured all over Italy, comes from here. The sauce is of fried pieces of bacon and raw beaten egg poured over the spaghetti while hot so that the egg cooks immediately.

Good white wines here, if a little thin – Frascati, Est! Est! Est! (both dry or sweet) and Nettuno (dry).

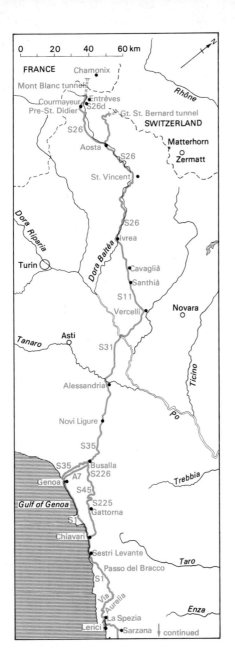

↓ continued

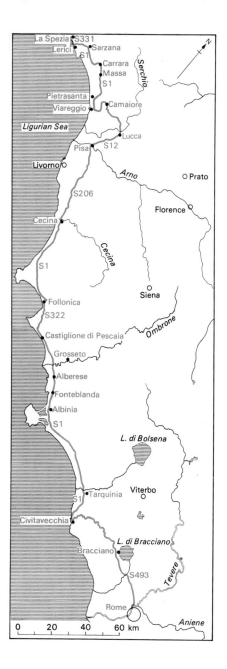

Route 1
Mont Blanc tunnel/
Great St Bernard
to Rome
(via Pisa)

Mont Blanc
tunnel 11.6 km
long, from
Chamonix (Les
Pélenis), France,
to Entrèves, Italy

(or the Great St
Bernard tunnel
and pass from
Switzerland)

S26d to
Courmayeur (4
km)

Entrèves – Maison de
Filippo: famous for local
dishes from local
ingredients, fine baked ham,
fonduta (fondue with local
cheese, eggs, butter and
milk), served with polenta, a
maize bread, beef stew, and
mountain game, including
chamois. Mountainous
meals for mountain men.
Antipasto is unusual and
good. Closed mid-June to
mid-July, and Tuesdays.
Meals L10,000–16,000.

You are in the Aosta valley,
with some of the most
impressive scenery in Italy
and four of the tallest peaks
in Europe: Mont Blanc,
Matterhorn (Cervin), Monta
Rosa and Gran Paradiso.
Once part of Savoy, now a
self-administering district
whose people send
members to Italy's
parliament but mostly
speak French, especially in
mountain villages.

Courmayeur – K2, via Val Sapin, Villair: most friendly restaurant on two floors, one traditional, the other almost rustic local. Speciality: Pollo K2, boned chicken stuffed with bacon; good desserts. Meals L10,500–12,000, excellent value. Good wine list. Closed Mondays and November.

Petite Bouffe, via della Vittorio, Dolonne: 16th-century house in old village; *albergo,* restaurant and disco; pleasant, cheapish; meals L10,000–12,000.

Le Vieux Pommier, piazza a Monte Bianco: good value; try dishes with local beef. Meals L8,000–10,000. Closed Mondays and October.

Good choice of hotels, *pensioni* and *alberghi:*

Hotel Vittoria: one of the oldest, just nicely modernized inside; rooms L26,000–29,000.

Nice *pensioni* are: Turistica, with good food; Joli at La Palud, run by Giorgio Perrod of Piccolo Padre restaurant; Pension Busa in old town.

Courmayeur, always fashionable with the rich, has become popular for winter and summer holidays since the opening of Mont Blanc tunnel (1965). If you left anything behind in France, just take the cable car from La Palud to Hellbronner, telecabin to Aiguille du Midi, then cable car to Chamonix and you are on the French side of Mont Blanc – a sensational journey.

Magnificent views (when clear!) from top cable car station of Cresta d'Arp 2,720 m (9,065 ft) – return fare L2,800. Little resort and spa at 995 m (3,315 ft); chalybeate springs; 11th-century Romanesque church tower; baroque altar.

S26d	Hotel Bellevue, via Monte
Pre Saint Didier	Bianco: truly *belle* views of
(5 km)	Monte Bianco and excellent

S26d Pre Saint Didier (5 km)

Hotel Bellevue, via Monte Bianco: truly *belle* views of Monte Bianco and excellent value; try local beef casserole (carbonada alla valdostana), lamb and beautiful cannelloni. Meals L8,000-10,000. Closed Tuesdays.

S26 Aosta (35 km)

Valle d'Aosta Hotel, Corso Ivrea: owned by Rank; handsome décor, splendid views; pricy, but value. Meals L13,000-20,000; rooms L35,000-50,000.

Cavallo Bianco, via Aubert: good food in a nice atmosphere; try Ueca soup, hot antipasto, and steak valdostana – with a herby butter and lemon sauce; fine wine list, with all local wines and good range from round Italy. Meals L13,000-15,000. Closed Mondays, Sunday evenings.

Rayon du Soleil, 2 km along S27: in garden; nice views; sound–proofed rooms. Good cooking: try agnolotti (variety of ravioli filled with beef, spinach, egg, cheese and nutmeg). Meals L7,300-14,000; closed 15 Nov. to 15 Mar.; rooms L14,000–24,000.

Mignon, strada del Gran San Bernado: comfortable rooms L12,000-20,000. No restaurant.

The road passes ruined castles which abound in Aosta valley, Alpine pastures sprinkled with sheep and cattle, old-time *raccards* of larchwood for hay, little villages with Alpine houses, and a backcloth of mountains, with views of Mont Blanc and its sister peaks. Vineyards begin at Morgex, where the church has a 17th-century fresco. Avise, photogenic little town, has three ruined castles. Just after Villeneuve are 13th-century Colin Tower (left) and Château de Sarriod (right). Then St Pierre village looms up with a square towered castle with round turrets. Augustus Caesar founded Aosta, and his Roman arch remains. St Anselm was born here and his house remains (in via San Anselmo). He is buried in Canterbury Cathedral, where he was archbishop from 1093, feuding with William Rufus and Henry I. Aosta Cathedral is a mixture of design from 12th to 19th centuries.

Collegiate Church, also with muddled architecture, has Romanesque cloisters with 12th-century carvings in marble of fables and biblical stories. Lime tree opposite is said to be 400 years old.

Cable car to Pila (one hour, return L2,000) gives fine views of Mont Blanc, Matterhorn and Monte Rosa.

**S26
St Vincent
(26 km)**

Le Grenier, piazza Zerbion: excellent value; superb risotto 'peasant style' with smoked sausage, white beans and mushrooms; try also gnocchi alla fontina (dumpling-like pasta poached in milk, rolled in cheese, then fried – very filling), and excellent crêpe Georgette (with pineapple, walnuts, cream and Grand Marnier). Meals L15,000–20,000. Closed Tuesdays, January and late July.

Batezar-da-Renato, via Marconi: pricy but good. Meals L20,000. Closed Wednesdays.

Pretty road past farms with chestnut and walnut trees, much nicer than the motorway. More castles on either side. Fenis (short road to left 12 km past Aosta) is worth visiting; lovely site; fine chapel wall-paintings of saints and sages with baffling proverbs in old French; rebuilt 1330, now contains interesting old furniture. Closed Tuesdays.

Like most small spas, St Vincent is neat and elegant with fine parks and a casino where gambling is heavy, so you can trim your figure and bank balance simultaneously. Spring waters contain bromine, bicarbonate and sulphate and are used for treating liver and stomach complaints, including obesity and indigestion.

S26 Ivrea (45 km)	At Lake Sirio, 2 km north – Hotel Sirio: famous for its mixed grill (includes pork and veal cutlets, various sausages, kidney, liver, game birds and lamb cutlets). Good risotto, too, and lake trout. Meals L9,000-16,000. I had a good local Carema wine, a fairly heavy red. Rooms L14,500-32,000.	Beautiful stretch of road with charming villages and farms. Just past Verres (15 km) road to right leads to Issogne castle, 15th-century courtyard with fountains and brightly painted walls. Worth seeing. Arnaz is a quaint medieval village. Bard, also medieval with 13th- to 16th-century houses, has a huge fortress, dismantled by Napoleon, rebuilt. Ivrea is in Piedmont – a lively market town with industries, including huge Olivetti calculating machine and typewriter factory.
S228 to Cavaglia, Santhia S11 to Vercelli (48 km)	At Santhia – San Massimo: reasonably priced restaurant with some cheap rooms. Meals L7,000-11,000. Closed Fridays. Rooms L7,000-17,000.	Rice-growing area; Vercelli has quiet old quarters.
S31 Alessandria (54 km)	Several good restaurants – Alli Due Buoi Rossi, via Cavour: *really* good; reasonable prices. Excellent bagna cauda (dip of hot olive oil, garlic, and cream, into which you plunge vegetables); good agnolotti pasta; bollito misto (mixed hot meats – beef, chicken, sausage, pork, with vegetables and a sharp green sauce – very tasty); spumone (fresh fruit ice cream with nuts). Nice atmosphere; good wines of	Famous for Borsolino hats; lively little place with medieval buildings and new industries.

Piedmont – fine Barolo red, drier and less mature Barbaresco, and acidic Barbera, which goes well with richer dishes. Meals at L9,000-10,000 are excellent value; pay L15,000 and value is still good. Closed, alas, in August.

Lux Hotel, via Piacenza: comfortable overnight stop; air conditioning; no restaurant. Rooms L15,000-35,000.

S35b to Novi Ligure, S35 to Bussala, then S226, S45, S225, via Gattorna, Carasco, then sharp right to reach coast at Chiavari (140 km)

Chiavari – Lord Nelson Pub, corso Valparaiso: France's *Michelin Guide* gives it a star for cooking; Napoleon must be revolving in his grave. Spaghetti alla Nelson, fillet steak alla Nelson; aragosta all'ammiraglia (lobster of the admiral); but you cannot turn a blind eye to the price. Meals L16,000-25,000. Closed Mondays. No rooms, but 160 brands of whisky and 30 marks of champagne.

Monterosa, via Monsignor Marinetti: large hotel in quiet spot; restaurant is good value: magnificent cappon magro salad, veal in green sauce, minestrone. Meals L8,000-12,000. Closed Mondays. Rooms L12,000-19,000.

Hill route missing Genoa and almost free of lorries and holiday traffic. Real farming country with working villages, but mountains obscure the sea.

Chiavari is industrial but neat, with flower-lined wide avenues. Lavagna, resort with rather scruffy beach, across river. Chiavari was home of Italian organ-grinders and men who built Peru. Museum has priceless Inca treasures. Old arcaded streets behind citadel; cathedral's fake front imitates Rome's Pantheon. Craftsmen make lovely furniture, also macramé towels of Arab origin with knotted fringes.

alternative route through Genoa (Genova) from Busalla (61 km from Alessandria)

S35 to Genoa (25 km) or A7 motorway (20 km)

S1 along coast to Chiavari (38 km)

Genoa – old fishermen's taverns still open on waterfront, selling tasty fish dishes, heavily herbed, and local white wine, often from bare tables.

Try burrida, Italy's fish soup originating here. Antica Osteria Pacetti, Borgo Incrociate: true Genoese dishes including prawns, shrimps, mussels; try cappon magro, meaning 'lean capon', joke name for a salad of eggs, vegetables, fish and shellfish in a sharp green sauce. Meals L9,000-14,000; good wine choice. Ornella and Renato Pacetti are world-known chefs. Closed Mondays and July.

Trattoria del Mario, via Conservatori del Mare: fashionable but superb cooking; fine fish soup and fish antipasto. I love trenetto del pesto (local spaghetti in a sauce of garlic, cheese, olive oil and basil, the local herb). Meals L13,000-15,000; closed Saturdays.

Genoa's traffic can be temper-destroying and coast traffic almost as bad. Among industrial wastelands Genoa has many fine things: narrow alleys *(carrugi)* near the port with interesting shops and expert pickpockets; via Balbi, one of Italy's finest streets, lined with old palaces, including royal palace (fine furnishing, mirror gallery, Van Dyck paintings); 17th-century Palazzo Durazzi (more Van Dyck); most unusual cathedral (San Lorenzo) – Gothic style in black and white marble; Banco San Giorgio on waterfront made from stone brought from Venice by sea in the 13th century, was long HQ of famous Genoese Bank.

Along S45 (1½ km) is Staglieno cemetery with remarkable and ostentatious tomb architecture. Along this route you go through Rapallo, near to the smart resorts of Santa Margherita and Portofino – beautiful, dear and hopelessly crowded.

Sestri Levante
(10 km)

Portobello, Baia del Silenzio: beach view, real local fish dishes – fresh anchovies (acciughe); prawns and squid grilled on skewers (spiedini di gamberi e totani); fine fish soup; battarga (starter made from tunny and grey mullet roe). Meals L10,000–14,000. Closed Mondays.

Carmagnini, lungomare De Scalzo: not cheap but one of the best restaurants on the coast. Friendly, good service and choice, fine cooking; try risotto; spaghetti with shellfish sauce; lobster aragosta; soup with datteri (*not* dates – small mussels!); fish; mixed grill. Well-chosen wine list includes a frizzante (slightly fermenting); pale, subtle and bright Vermentino. Meals L15,000-20,000. Sea views. Closed Tuesdays and January.

Beautifully sited on a rocky peninsula with soft sand beaches and a wooded area which is now the park of Grand Hotel dei Castelli. Dante sang its praises. I would if I could sing.

S1 via Aurelia through Passo del Bracco, Pian di Barca to La Spezia (59 km)

La Spezia: not a great place to stay, but these are fair value – La Posta restaurant, via Don Minzoni: good food. Meals L9,000 (tourist menu)-12,000. Closed Saturdays and Sundays.

Hotel Diana, via Colombo: no restaurant; small, fairly comfortable. Rooms L14,000-18,000. Singles L7,750.

Portovenere (nicer spot for an overnight) – Locanda San Pietro: fine view of gulf; comfortable. Meals L10,000-15,000. Fresh fish landed daily. Half-*pensione* L30,000 per person.

Le Grazie (3 km) – Da Pietro il Palombaro: superb fish caught by the owner, cooked by his wife; good value.

This attractive route through a 2,000 ft pass, once plagued with traffic, is almost peaceful now that the motorway takes traffic from Genoa to Pisa and Livorno. Breathtaking views of the Bay of Spezia, almost landlocked and backed by tiers of wooded hills. Beyond, you see the marble mountain of Carrara. Below, along coast lie the Cinque Terre (Five Lands), medieval fishing villages backed by steep terraced hills growing grapes for strong sweet wine. Once linked only by mule tracks, sea or rail; now a road of sorts links the route with Monterosso, another from just south of La Spezia to Riomaggiore; new corniche road (La Spezia to Sestri Levante) already reaches Manorola.

Vernassa is prettiest – forts, bell towers, old buildings lining tiny squares and narrow streets. Well worth a diversion if time permits, but do not miss Bracco Pass. La Spezia, naval port with one of world's best natural harbours. Modern industrial but white houses, gardens, palms and pines. Portovenere (fishing village with mussel beds, 12 km along pretty corniche road) is most attractive; dominated by old citadel; 12th-century houses along port, steep alleys with stairs; 12th-century church on rock made partly from black marble streaked orange and yellow, quarried on offshore isles. Below it is Byron's Cave, with inscription saying that he found inspiration for his poem 'The Corsair' here and reminding of his swim from Lerici, across the bay.

S331 Lerici (10 km) then inland to Sarzana (7 km)

Lerici – Hotel Panoramic, Fiascherino: good value but open only March–mid-October. Meals L8,500-11,500; rooms L12,000-16,000.

Byron, lungomare Biaggini: small, sea views, comfortable; medium prices.

La Calata, via Mazzini: near port; excellent fish and shellfish; nautical décor. Meals L10,000-15,000. Closed Mondays.

Conchiglia, piazza del Molo: one of my favourites; genuine and good regional cooking; try ravioli with seafood; spaghetti con uove di pesce (with roe); branzino (sea bass). Owner Massimo Lorato's pride is his risotto with seafood and roe; unusual local white wine called Linero. Meals around L12,000 but can be much cheaper. Closed Wednesdays and October.

Just before Lerici is San Terenzo, with castle on headland and Casa Magni, white villa with arcades; here the Shelleys, Byron and Trelawny – his ex-pirate friend – spent the unhappy summer of 1822; Shelley was drowned when his yacht capsized in a storm near Viareggio. Lerici's 16th-century castle, with shining strips of black and white stone, dominates the medieval old town.

Fiascerino, 3 km from Lerici, has pines down to the water; was called by D. H. Lawrence 'one of the most beautiful places in the world'. Still beautiful.

Sarzana, fortified town on river with ramparts intact and superb triangular fortress with baroque and rococo towers. Home of Buonaparte family before they emigrated to Corsica.

S1 to Luni (10 km)
then local road
left to Carrara in
Tuscany (6 km)

Luni: remains of Roman amphitheatre, basilica and baths; newly found altar to moon worship is of uncertain period. Cities of Luni and Lucca once both laid claim to a wooden face of Christ, found floating in the sea – Volto Santo, said to have been made by Nicodemus after Calvary. It was put in an unattended ox cart and left to the oxen. They took it to Lucca, where it rests in the cathedral.

Carrara: marble quarries on mountainside were used by the Romans; Michelangelo came to pick the stone for his sculptures; Henry Moore had a studio here. Studios along the road where local craftsmen make and sell small statues. Watch the marble cut by wires like huge pieces of cheese.

local road to Massa (7 km)

Fiorentino, via Democrazia: very good value; try tortelli – like a ravioli filled with cheese and spinach; meals L6,000-8,000. Closed Saturdays.

Marina di Massa – Residenza Marina, via Magliano: little hotel, excellent value, but open only May-October. Rooms L25,000. Meals L10,000. Nice garden; quiet; own parking.

Narrow streets of old Massa lead to Rocca, 15th-century palace of the old rulers, the Malaspinas. Many famous people were guests here.

Very attractive main square with orange trees, flagstone paving, three 13th-century Romanesque buildings, and fine cathedral. Ducal palace, now police station, has a nice courtyard with loggia and Neptune's statue.

Marina di Massa (5 km) – elegant resort has now become again an important port. Strange piece of 'Mussolini style' architecture is the Fiat Tower, built as a holiday centre for workers.

S1 Pietrasanta (11 km)

Pietrasanta means 'holy stone'. From here Michelangelo built a road up to Monte Altissimo to transport white marble for his statue 'Pietà', now in St Peter's Basilica in the Vatican. Beach resort Marina di Pietrasanta has good sands.

S1 Viareggio (8 km)

Good place for eating, with Tuscan dishes; *Michelin* stars three restaurants – all good, but I prefer some others.

Genny, via G. Zanardelli: lively almost eccentric;

Rebuilt in a hurry after war damage, far from handsome, still fashionable but popular also. Lively and grows on you. Active working port where fishing boats jostle expensive

huge hors d'oeuvre table; excellent spaghetti allo scoglio (mixed local shellfish) and spaghetti alla puttaniara (which you can translate either as 'noisy and quarrelsome' or 'in the manner of a brothel', and which has a powerful sauce of hot peppers, garlic, tomatoes and olives); wonderful fish fresh from the port; scampi cooked many ways, including in brandy; digestive grappa with a smooth kick. House wines are Montecarlo white and red from Lucca. Meals excellent value at L12,000-14,000 (book in high season – tel. 45548). Closed Tuesdays and November. Attached Hotel Mirage: rooms L27,000 (L17,000 single).

Fedi, via
Verdi: locals love the 'simple' cooking of Gianfranco Francesconi, patron chef. Fresh local fish dishes such as superb fried mussels and little prawns (gamberetti), big prawns (gamberoni) grilled, scampi and whatever good fish that is landed in the port that morning, fried in breadcrumbs, baked or grilled. Excellent desserts. Meals L12,000-14,000. Closed Tuesdays except midsummer.

Margherita, Lungomare Margherita: once a smart dine and dance with cabaret restaurant where yachts; nice shops on promenade; peace in extensive pine woods each side. Good sands where Shelley's body was washed up after his yacht sank.

At Torre del Lago, Lake Massacuccoli (5 km south-east) is Puccini's villa (open to the public) where he wrote *La Bohème*.

Puccini met Toscanini. Now a good popular restaurant with a pizzeria attached in which genuine fresh pizza are made in an open oven, the real way. Restaurant has a huge antipasto table, laden with everything from asparagus to lobster; serves good risotto, superb baked fish. I have had the excellent traditional dish of viareggio – spaghetti con le telline (with cockles, garlic, tomatoes and peppers). Meals L9,000-13,000. House wine costs L3,000 but is high quality. Closed Wednesdays except in July and August.

Olivo Aldo, viale Margherita (by Bagno Balena): nice friendly little restaurant where I have had many good meals; even the house dog is really welcoming. Good plain cooking and very good value; try tortellini (pasta rings stuffed with veal, chicken and cheese and probably the best pasta made). Meals L8,000-10,000.

Hotels of all types. Try: Garden, via Ugo Foxola: recently renovated; same owners for 21 years. Rooms L18,000-30,000; meals L8,000-13,000.

Excelsior, on promenade: well-run but not all rooms have baths; moderate prices.

Viareggio
continued

Albergo Bella Riviera, on promenade, Viale Manin: simple, almost basic but very convenient. Rooms with bath L10,000–15,000. One of the oldest *alberghi* in town.

local road through Camaiore to Lucca (29 km) (or motorway if in a hurry)

Buca di Sant'Antonio, via della Cervia: remarkably good value; excellent risotto; pappardelle alla lepre (local pasta with rich hare sauce); roast kid (tastes rather like stronger veal); local Montecarlo wine. Meals L9,000–12,000. Closed Mondays, Sunday evenings, and late July. Coaching inn from 1800.

Sergio, piazza dei Bernardini: good food, excellent service, smart. L8,000–14,000. Closed Tuesdays.

Pizzeria Pacini, piazza Napoleone: watch Eugenio Pacini, master of the pizza, making his masterpieces, then cooking them in the open oven. Try any of the varieties and you may never buy another 'plastic' pizza. I had one ten inches across, containing about ¼ lb ham, for L1,300.

Lucca is one of the finest medieval cities in Europe – do not miss it. One of my favourite old cities because it has little traffic compared with many places and fewer tourists. It is surrounded by ramparts so wide that they are lined with trees and have a promenade around them. The narrow streets and tiny squares are charming and the old city is small enough to wander round and enjoy.

Fine old palaces, shops and towers in red brick. Volto Santo (see Luni) found in the sea is in the 13th-century cathedral, which is of brilliantly coloured marble. Lucca was once one of the great cities of Europe, fighting constantly for its independence.

One small piazza hides Lucca's most historic building, the church of San Frediano. He was an Irishman, called Finnian because of his fair hair. Frediano is the Italian equivalent. Sent to a monastery at Dromore, he made a pilgrimage to Rome, on his way performing a quick miracle in Ayrshire by diverting a river. He did the same in Lucca to save it from flooding, returned to Ireland to convert those whom St Patrick had missed, then went back to Lucca to become bishop. He was helped in his miracles by having been trained in bridge and embankment building. His church has fine Roman columns and carvings looted from earlier buildings. There are also superb Christian sculptures and the grave of a mysterious St Richard, King of England, who is said to have been a prince from Devon who died on a pilgrimage to Rome.

The centre of Lucca is a big square called piazza Napoleone, after Napoleon's sister Elisa who, as Princess of Lucca, ruled the town strongly but rather well. She took great interest in the arts and even greater in young artists! Her sister was Pauline Borghese, Napoleon's favourite sister and is the beauty lying on a couch sculptured by Canova (Borghese Palace, Rome). A spoilt girl whose extravagant ways partly caused the people of Haiti to revolt, she died here in exile.

S12b
Pisa
(22 km)

This is the best way to approach this compact, charming city. You see the red walls, then the tops of the Leaning Tower, the baptistry dome, and finally the cupola of the cathedral. They are grouped photogenically and conveniently together in the piazza del Duomo, and are floodlit at night in a strange greenish light. In sunlight their white marble glows. Across the square is the remarkable 12th-century cemetery, Campo Santo.

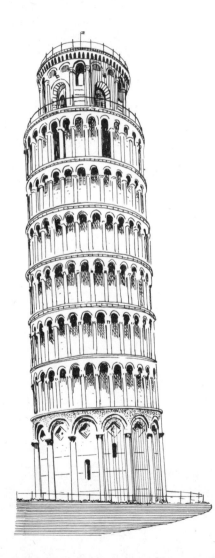

The Leaning Tower, a belfry built of white marble in the Romanesque style, is to me the most beautiful of the group. Some tourists are so bemused by its angle that they miss the tiers of slender pillars and rounded arches. It was begun in 1164 by Bonano Pisano, one of a family of sculptor-architects. It seems to have been abandoned after foundations sunk on one side, but was completed between 1275 and 1350. As it weighs 15,000 tons, its continued existence is remarkable. You can walk up the 294 steps for a panorama of Pisa, but some say the dipping stairs make them seasick. The story goes that the astronomer and physicist Galileo, a local lad, used the tower for working out his principle of the acceleration of falling bodies, and invented the pendulum clock after seeing a bronze lamp swinging in the nearby cathedral, but modern pedants argue against this. I prefer a good story to an argument.

The cathedral (1068–1118), in marble of alternating colours, looks almost delicate from outside but vast as you enter. There are sixty-eight single columns. Giovanni Pisano's pulpit is considered by those who know more than I do about sculpture to be even more magnificent than the pulpit his father Nicolo designed in 1206 for the neighbouring baptistry. Alas, Giovanni's was reconstructed in 1926 after a fire. The round marble baptistry has a 13th-century font, once used for baptisms by immersion.

The Campo Santo cemetery is beautiful and too old to be macabre. During Hitler's war, the Germans were on the north side of the river Arno in Pisa, the Allies on the south, and it is surprising how little damage was done to this piazza by bombs and shellfire. Shells and fire destroyed some of the greatest frescos of Campo Santo. But others have been beautifully restored. The cemetery was founded by Crusaders who brought back soil from the Hill of Calvary at Jerusalem, and the Gothic galleries are paved with 600 tombstones. A huge chain once protected Pisa harbour against invaders but in 1284 the Genoese defeated the Pisan navy, took away the chain and ended Pisa's rivalry with Genoa and Venice for mastery of the Mediterranean. Pisa got its chain back when Italy was united in 1860, but the river Arno estuary had silted up and Pisa was far from the sea.

Piazza dei Cavalieri, between the Leaning Tower and river, is splendid, with a kaleidoscope of architecture from several centuries. The Church of St Stephen was built in

Pisa
continued

the 16th century by Grand Duke Cosimo de Medici for his
new military order, the Knights of St Stephen, which he
created to fight the Saracen raiders; he was short of
knights because he had eliminated or banished most of
them. Take a slow walk along each bank of the Arno river.
Park when you can and walk; parking is a real problem.
Most likely spots are by the station or by the cathedral.

Restaurants and hotels
Arno Hotel and Antonio Restaurant, piazza della
Repubblica: a little gem, one of my favourites in Italy and
the nearest I know in Italy to a French 3-star *logis.* Hidden
in the corner of the square which contains the law courts;
therefore there is parking when the law courts are closed.
Pretty bedrooms. Excellent food and cooking. Try genuine
'rustico' prosciutto crudo – real country-cured ham, not the
more delicate Parma or San Daniele ham of gourmets; I
prefer it. Superb home-made tagliatelle pasta, with a
choice of sauces; so is veal in cream and wine sauce. But
Antonio Pianigiano has a fine menu – enough dishes to find
what you want and eat a balanced meal, not so many that
you know some cannot be freshly made. You can have a
good three-course meal for L8,000. I paid L12,000 for a
four-course meal, including a bottle of Brolio Ricasole
Classico '73 (one of the best wines in Italy). The wine list is
good and the house wine costs L1,500. Chianti Classico
Villa Antinori is excellent. Not even French restaurants can
offer better value. Rooms L18,000-30,000. Telephone
ahead: 22243/40986 Pisa.

Royal Hotel Victoria, lungarno Pacinotti: on south riverside;
looks like its name but has nice décor and some beautiful
bedrooms. I recommend the restaurant; menu L6,700;
garage. Rooms L11,000-28,000.

Hotel Duome, via Santa Maria: useful modern
air-conditioned hotel near Leaning Tower. Efficient rather
than friendly. Rooms L28,000-46,000. Garage (small). I
have not tried the restaurant. Meals L11,500.

Santa Maria, via Santa Maria: a few steps from Leaning
Tower; two restaurants, one self-service, one waiter-
service. Waiter-service meals L9,000-13,000; tourist
menu (3 course) L5,500. Closed Mondays.

Many cheap restaurants between station and piazza
Vittorio Emanuele in small side streets.

Sergio, lungarno Pacinotti: fine meals at a price; owner-chef Sergio Lorenzi is an enthusiast and famous in Italy. Meals L15,000-25,000. Closed 10-25 July.

S206 Cecina (55 km) join S1 to Follonica (55 km)	6 km past Follonica, at Puntone Scarlino – Cala Felice: country restaurant with L12,000 menu including wine; open June-September.	Industrial road at first, but missing the industrial city of Livorno. Marina di Cecina (3 km) is a small beach resort with dark sands. Scenery improves fast and becomes delightful, with pine woods.
S322 Castiglione della Pescaia (23 km)	Trattoria Antonietta, via Colombo: quayside trattoria found by tourists but still genuine. Animated terrace, cosy interior: try fish salad with dishes made from local shellfish; excellent fritto misto of shellfish and small red mullet, fried; fish grilled over charcoal; tagliatelle pasta with shellfish sauce – in fact, any fish. Good-value meals. I had three courses for L7,000. A litre of good Tuscan wine costs L3,000. Closed Tuesdays. Restaurant da Romolo, corsa della Liberta: splendid spaghetti and locally caught fish, especially shellfish. Meals around L15,000. Closed Tuesdays. Hotel Roma, via Colombo: facing harbour with back entrance into little square. Comfortable, central, sun-patio roof with harbour views. A nice hotel. Meals around L8,000; rooms L20,000-29,000.	Castiglione is a charming old fishing town becoming a little too popular mid-summer through invasion of yachtsmen, but good fun. Good new car park. Working fishing fleet. Freshly landed fish sold from stalls along the promenade. Two good beaches.

S322 to a
junction where
left road leads to
Grosseto, right
road to Marina di
Grosseto; we
drive straight on –
a local road to
Trappola and
Alberese (15 km)

drive through
nature reserve
rejoining S1 at
Collechio (6 km)

S1 to Fonteblanda
and Albinia
(16 km)

Albinia – De Renata: pleasant restaurant with rooms. Meals L8,000-12,000. Rooms L11,000-19,000.

At Port 'Ercole (Monte Argentario) – Al Gambero Rosso, lungomare Andrea Doria: on terrace in front of port; good plain cooking of seafood; try scampi, fish soup and conchiglie. Meals L10,000-12,000. Closed Thursdays, November and December.

At Ansedonia – Il Pescatore, via della Tagliata: excellent but pricy. Outstanding fish soup and fish risotto; good fresh white fish, grilled or baked and served with a most unusual green sauce mixed with mayonnaise, brandy and herbs. Some think this to be one of Italy's best fish restaurants. Meals L12,000-16,000. Closed Tuesdays.

Route goes through pine woods, then over the river Ombrone into the nature park. Once this area, the Maremma, was a mosquito-ridden wooded swamp. Malaria drove the people away most of the year, only shepherds and bandits who raided the empty villages stayed behind, and Dante used it in his *Inferno* as the inferno woods. Now it is drained, sheep graze in lush pastures and wild boar and roebuck live in the woods. From Fonteblanda, a little road leads to Talamone, founded by one of the Argonauts; it has strong walls, partly Roman. Barbarossa, corsair and admiral of the Turkish empire, when he landed in the 16th century, ordered the killing of the whole population except for one lovely girl, Margherita, whom he took back for the harem of Suliman the Magnificent. She became Suliman's favourite wife and a political power. Garibaldi landed here, too – in 1860 to collect arms for his freedom fighters.

Left from Albinia is Magliano (15 km), a medieval city still complete with ramparts, bastions and towers, old houses, photogenic streets; it is little known to tourists.

A road between sea and lagoon from Albinia leads to Orbetello on a strip of land joining Monte Argentario to mainland at Ansedonia, ruined Roman city. Orbetello's walls are said to have been built by the Etruscans. Try not to miss it.

S1 Tarquinia (59 km)

Hotel Tarconte, via Tuscia: modern, comfortable, good service; panoramic views. Rooms L12,000-22,000. Attached is Solengo restaurant, excellent value. Meals L8,000-14,000.

At Marina di Tarquinia – Velcamare: excellent fish and lamb with local mushrooms; at the beach; twenty simple rooms L8,000-12,000 (higher prices are for July and August); meals L8,000-12,000.

A road from S1 winds up a hillside (3 km) to this delightful old city of towers, yellow-grey walls, battlements, old palaces and narrow streets; the Romans called it Corneto and it ruled the whole coast area. Before that, it was the capital city of the Etruscans, the mystery people who finally fell to the Romans and were absorbed. From them the Romans took their laws, some of their gods, and their gladiatorial combats. The Etruscans were artisans and technicians, mining iron, copper and silver and trading extensively. Their zenith was during 7th-8th centuries BC. In Palazzo Vitelleschi, a 15th-century Gothic cardinal's palace with pretty windows, is a museum of Etruscan remains, including winged horses, charming jewellery, vases and urns with satyrs, lively-looking nymphs and muscular heroes reminiscent of the Greeks. Here too are frescos showing the rape of

Tarquinia
continued

Lucretia by King Tarquin.
Tarquinia provided the first
two Roman kings – Tarquin
the Ancient and Tarquin the
Proud. The rape of Lucretia
by the latter's son brought
about the fall of the great
House of Tarquin.

Etruscan burial ground near
by, the necropolis, built like
a town. Thousands of
tombs stretch for 5 km, and
you can see the important
ones with remarkable wall
paintings showing people
dancing, drinking, hunting,
fishing, playing games and
acting plays; sexy and
earthy, and all in five
colours. Well worth seeing,
though it takes two hours
and you must apply at the
museum to join a guided car
convoy.

S1 Civitavecchia
(20 km) then
inland on winding
but pleasant road
to meet the via
Claudia (S493);
turn right and
later left for
Bracciano on
Lake Bracciano
(53 km)

Bracciano – Casina del
Lago, lungolago: pleasant
lake views; good country
cooking; try lake eels and
trote (small trout sauté)
with bay leaves and onion;
good cannelloni. Meals
L10,000-15,000; twelve
rooms around L10,000-
15,000. Closed Tuesdays.

Civitavecchia, port of
Rome, is not very attractive.
Stendhal lived here as
French consul and wrote
Chartreuse of Parma.
Bracciano is a pleasant lake
resort a short way from the
lake which is surrounded
by green hills planted with
olives and pines. Town built
round a castle built in 15th
century by the Orsini family,
now owned by Prince
Odescalchi; there are
guided tours Thursdays,
Saturdays and Sundays.
Beautiful furnishings. You
can swim from the
organized lake beach, but it
is packed with Romans on
summer weekends.

S493 to Rome
(50 km)

Route 2
Simplon Pass/rail
tunnel to Rome
(via Milan, Bologna, Florence, Siena)

This is the art-lovers' road to Rome, with visits to Florence and Siena, but there is plenty along the route for others – mountain scenery after the Simplon Pass, magnificent scenery between Bologna and Florence, the resorts of Lake Maggiore, and some of the best food in Europe – around Parma and Bologna and again in Tuscany around Florence and Siena.

The difficult decision is – how long to spend in Florence? A week would not be too much for most people, a year too little for some. Mind you, the noise and traffic muddle might drive you out more quickly. But you must save time for Siena, where you need at least a day and a night simply to absorb the charming atmosphere. Viterbo is interesting and charming, too – although when I was last there the BBC were shooting a TV film about the abominable Borgias!

Our Bologna–Florence run over the Futa Pass is simply magnificent, but if time or weariness makes you take to the motorway, you have a consolation – it's one of the most scenic stretches of motorway in Europe.

As far as Bologna, this is also the route to the Adriatic resorts of Rimini, Cattolica, Pesaro and Ricchione. The stretch is included at the end of the Rome route.

You can taste some superb dishes around Parma and Bologna. The Parma version of stracotto is topside stewed whole with wine, pork sausage, vegetables, cinnamon and other spices and herbs, garnished with mushrooms. Try also Bologna's canestrelli di pollo (chicken fillet stuffed with smoked ham and onion, served on spinach), budino di pollo in brodo (chicken soup served with a cream made from chicken purée, eggs and grated cheese), spella di San Secondo (shoulder of pork cured like ham), lasagne al forno (the baked pasta dish so superb in Bologna, so awful sometimes in Britain or from a deep-freeze packet), Parma ham (though many Italians think San Daniele ham from Udine is even better), parmigiano cheese (parmesan, which is not only grated but eaten when young and chewable and goes superbly with wine) and, of course, the greatest of pasta dishes, tortellini alla Bolognese.

This is the land of Lambrusco, the refreshing, *pétillant* weakish red wine which fizzes slightly and is more of a thirst-quencher than a dinner wine.

Save some of your appetite for Florence. The Florentines claim to have started French cuisine when Catherine de Medici, married to Henry II, brought to Paris her Florentine cooks, their recipes and even the ingredients.

Apart from Tuscan dishes mentioned in Route 1, try arista alla Fiorentina (saddle of pork, seasoned with rosemary and garlic, baked *gently* in the oven); Siena's buristo suino (rich pork casserole with raisins and pine nuts); trippa alla Fiorentina (strips of tripe cooked in meat and tomato sauce, served with grated parmesan); fritto misto alla Fiorentina (fried calves' brains, sweetbreads, chicken, artichoke hearts and mozzarella cheese), and Siena's copate (wafers of honey and nuts).

If you use the Mont Blanc crossing into Italy, simply follow Route 1 to just before Vercelli and join this route at Milan.

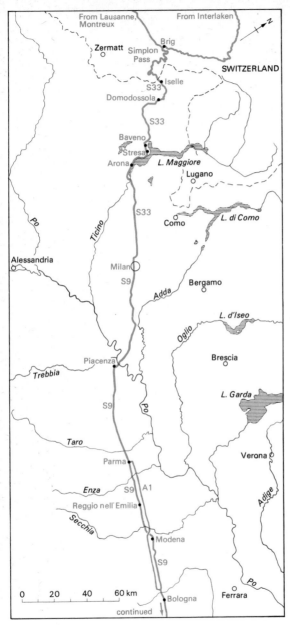

continued

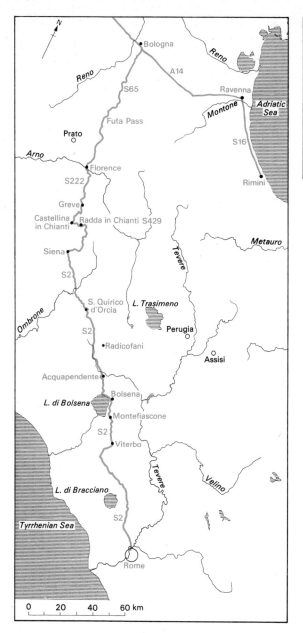

Route 2
Simplon Pass/rail
tunnel to Rome
(via Milan, Bologna, Florence, Siena)

Coming to the Simplon Pass (occasionally closed between November and April, reconstructed modern, 21 km long, rising continuously to summit) from Lausanne and Montreux or Interlaken on other side; or alternative all-year Simplon car-carrying rail tunnel (frequent services, 15-20 minutes): both from Brig in Switzerland, entering Italy at Iselle, then S33 to Domodossola (16 km) and on to Baveno (37 km)

Simplon not difficult but does rise from 680 m (2,231 ft) at Brig to 2,005 m (6,578 ft); winding lumpy road in Italy to Domodossola at 275 m (900 ft).

Baveno: I have no personal experience of Baveno's restaurants, but this has been recommended to me – Ripa: garden overlooking lake towards islands; meals L7,000-8,000; rooms L8,000-18,000; open April –September.

Queen Victoria stayed here. Water from the springs is recommended for gout. Quiet, still elegant resort on Lake Maggiore, which is 64 km (40 miles) long and has its top end in Switzerland. Old alleys and English-style Villa Branca, called Villa

Clara when Victoria stayed there in 1873. Baveno's gardens grow semi-tropical flowers. In the lake are the interesting Borromean Isles reached by boat in twenty minutes. Isola Pescatore and Isola Bella where the 17th-century palace has extraordinary gardens – beautiful views, unusual plants and aromatic herbs on the terraces, with garish statues. Pescatore is preserved like an old fishing village and is charming. The Borromeo family have owned the isles since the 12th century.

S33 Stresa (7 km)

Stresa – Emiliano, corso Italiano: best known restaurant, dull décor, excellent food, pricy. Good grill of lake fish, risotto; salmon; tortelloni di ricotta (large ravioli filled with cream cheese). Meals L15,000-25,000. Closed Tuesdays.

La Barchetta, via Garibaldi: very good value. Meals L10,000-12,000. Closed Wednesdays.

Ariston, corso Italia: small hotel serving good meals. Home-made pasta. Meals L9,000-14,000; rooms L9,000-15,000. Veranda overlooking lake.

Recommended for money-savers – Primavera, via Cavour: value for money; no restaurant; rooms L11,000 per person.

Stresa is the smart resort of Maggiore, with lovely villas and gardens, luxury, pricy hotels in the centre, nice small hotels towards outskirts. Reflection of the mountains and trees in the sunlit lake is a changing, fascinating scene. Lovely gardens to the Villa Ducale, once home of the philosopher Rosmini, and Villa Pallavincino park has llamas, ostriches, zebras and other animals under old trees, as well as fine views of lake and mountains (open April–October). Funicular to Monte Mottarone, with fine views; also by road, passing an interesting garden of Alpine plants.

Stresa
continued

At Someraro, 3 km north of Stresa: Auberge de la Chandelle: my favourite round here; country taverna with simple good dishes. Meals L11,000-15,000. Closed Mondays.

S33 Arona
(16 km)

Al Cantuccio, piazza del Popolo: sophisticated cooking; not cheap but good. Try veal cutlet al Cantuccio (with asparagus and gorgonzola). Meals from L10,500, but L15,000 more likely. Closed Tuesdays and part of August.

Pleasant little place by the lake with mountain background and lakeside walks.

S33 Milan
(64 km)

follow the signs for the A1 motorway in Milan and you will soon see signs also for via Emilia, S9

See Route 4.

Dull stretch, flat country, beginning of Milan industrial belt.

Piacenza
(68 km)

Piacenza is known for its pasta dishes, lasagne, ravioli tortelli (square cushions of pasta filled with cream cheese made from sheep's milk), cannelloni and gnocchi; also for turkey and guinea fowl baked in clay.
Danilo, corso Vittorio Emanuele: individualistic restaurant; good value, amusing lively atmosphere; country-cured ham, better salami, delicious genuine tortellini, queen of pasta. Good bean and bacon soup. Nice red house wine. Meals

Piacenza is not much visited by tourists, who make for Cremona, city of Stradivarius the violin maker. I like Piacenza – a typical, lively middle-sized trade centre with an old town of pleasant buildings and art treasures – unpretentious, friendly and not crammed with sightseers. You cross the river Po to enter through gates of old brick ramparts into streets often a bit dodgily narrow for modern traffic, and small squares. Until 1860 it was the border

L8,000-9,000. Closed Sundays.

Da Peppino, piazza San Antonio: I like it – variations on local dishes, well cooked and willingly served. Meals L8,000-12,000. Closed Thursdays and part of August.

Hotel Nazionale, via Genova 33: no restaurant, but a comfortable, fairly priced and convenient place to sleep. Garage under cover (L2,500). Rooms L16,000-23,000.

Agnello da Renato, via Calzolai: local institution; Renato Bandini keeps Piacenza's traditions alive

of the Hapsburg Empire and long before that a Roman outpost. Here Roman legions got caught between Hannibal and his brother's forces and were knee deep in the river when elephants were let loose on them. Not a pleasant day for them! In the main square, piazza Cavalli, is the impressive Gothic Palazzo del Commune (13th century) filling a whole side. The square is named after two horsemen's statues. San Francesco church, Romanesque-Gothic, is impressive: high on its bell-tower is an iron cage *gabbia* where people who had upset the establishment

Piacenza
continued

in his cooking and even, I am told, in his local dialect. Judging by the meals, he is justified. Meals L9,000–13,000. Closed Mondays and August.

used to be displayed naked to be mocked by the people. Times change. Nowadays some might be admired! The town museum was being transferred to Palazzo Farnese when I stayed there recently but it may be open by now and includes a famous 'Madonna' painted by Botticelli. A handsome modern art gallery, Ricci Oddi. After the Napoleonic wars, the city was ruled by Napoleon's wife Marie-Louise, ably assisted by a one-eyed lover, Count Neipberg. The fun of this place is just to watch the people going about their business and pleasure, especially early evening.

S9
Parma
(62 km)

Bologna is considered the greatest place to eat in this area but Parma challenges it. There are many great restaurants, and many good cheaper ones. These all serve the local dishes like bomba di riso (rice with pigeon), agnoloni (small ravioli filled with beef, pork and cheese), tortellini (round pasta stuffed with chicken, veal and cheese and truly a Bologna delicacy), tortelli alla parmigiana (square cushions of pasta filled with cottage cheese, spinach and parmesan, and nutmeg), parmesan cheese served young and soft and, of course, Parma ham, which should not only be

Known to us mostly for ham and cheese, but Toscanini was born here and Paganini buried here; art students love it because its art treasures cover so many periods and styles. The people are traditionally known for their gentility and refinement, and are therefore lampooned by inhabitants of lustier places. Has many good, though no really great, museums and old buildings. Toscanini's house (Borgo R. Tanzi 13) is a museum. In summer, sit outside a café in piazza Garibaldi and watch the beautiful women return from shopping expeditions in strada della Repubblica. Parma believes that it has

fresh-cut and succulent but have a sort of sharp-sweet taste.

Al Dsevd, via Bruno Longhi: try tortellini, pork. Meals around L12,000. Closed Mondays and part of August.

Angiol d'Or, via Scuttellari: try cannoli (pastry horns filled with cheese), beef and veal; lavish décor. Meals L13,000-17,000. Closed 15-30 August.

Aurora, vicolo San Alessandro: Margherita Montagna's restaurant still rates top with local people, even if not with *Michelin*. Pricy but very good. Try poultry in any form; good wine list. Meals L12,000-17,000. Closed Mondays and August.

La Filoma, strada XX Marzo: my favourite; simple décor, fine cooking. Try tortellini, tortelli alla parmigiana, stuffed veal, fresh parmesan; excellent wines, including Lambrusco and house red. Meals L10,000-15,000. Closed Wednesdays and July.

Hotel Bristol, strada Garibaldi: modern, good overnight pad; no restaurant; rooms L15,000-23,000.

Hotel Toscanini, viale Toscanini: comfortable hotel, good restaurant, called Torrente. Closed July. Meals L8,000-12,000; rooms L28,000-40,000.

the world's most beautiful women. Judge for yourself. Teatro Farnese, built 1619, based on Vicenza's Greek theatre, with colonnades and permanent scenery.

from Parma, you can take S9 to Reggio Emilia, and Modena to Bologna (91 km) but frankly it is not a very interesting stretch and you might as well take the Autostrada del Sole (A1) to Bologna (96 km)

Modena has one of Italy's finest art galleries, the Palazzo dei Musei, including works of El Greco, Veronese, Tintoretto, Bassano, Velasquez, and Flemish painters. Also a remarkable collection of medals, with mirrors showing their reverse side.

Bologna

Bologna claims to be the 'Lyon of Italian cuisine'. Though the boloney sausage originally came from Bologna, poor imitations have devalued it. The genuine local mortadella is still excellent. Tortellini alla Bolognese (pasta rings filled with veal, chicken and grated cheese, which should be cooked in chicken broth, perhaps with cream) is so good that Italian gourmets in Paris and London have it flown out to them. Try, too, tortelli, pappardelle verdi (flat pasta made with spinach served with rich sauce, often game), budino di pollo in brodo (chicken broth enriched with cream chicken purée), canestrelli di pollo (chicken fillet stuffed with smoked ham and onion, served on spinach), pasatelli in brodo (egg, breadcrumbs and cheese grated into a boiling chicken broth to make pasta lumps), turkey fillets grilled or in cream. Places to try them include:

Bologna is a big industrial city but has many treasures. Its history is almost that of Italy – founded as Felsina by Etruscans, taken by the Gauls, then by Romans, sacked by the northern 'barbarians', then in the 12th century involved in the factional power struggle between Guelphs and Ghibillines which tore central Italy apart. Now it is communist – but *Italian* communist. Old part is most attractive – red slate, beautiful use of rosy bricks, arcades, towers and domes. University, founded in AD 425, is still in the forefront of research in preventive medicine, and has an atomic research centre. In the 13th century it had a woman professor so lovely that she lectured from behind a curtain to avoid distracting her male students.

Piazza di Porta Ravegnana has *two* leaning towers: one built by Asinelli family in

Nettuno, via Laura Ferrati Bassi: excellent value, not cheap; good meat as well as pasta. Meals L9,000-13,000. Closed Mondays and late August.

All'Abadia, via dell'Abadia: excellent value; try game or poultry in cream. Meals L10,000-16,000. Closed Thursdays and August.

Grassili, via Dal Luzzo: very pricy and very good; unusual dishes include tagliatelle with smoked salmon, or with gorgonzola, tortellini and tortelloni (large ravioli) stuffed with egg, cream and mushrooms, splendid risotto and all traditional Bolognese dishes. Meals L16,000-20,000, but a culinary experience. Nice lesser-known wines. Closed Wednesdays and most of July.

Diana, via dell'Indipendenza: local dishes with a touch of individuality. Meals L11,000-15,000. Closed Mondays and August.

1109, 486 steps, 100 m (330 ft) high, with tilt of 2.3 m (7½ ft); and the other, Garisendo, 50 m (165 ft), leaning 3 m (10 ft). This square forms the centre with piazza del Nettuno (with the rather rugged Neptune fountain) and traffic-free piazza Maggiore with several treasures, including the Santo Stefano group of medieval churches and a complex of palaces – Palazzo Communale – with a good small art gallery. The archaeological museum (9 a.m. – 2 p.m., closed Mondays) is very interesting and includes Etruscan remains, as well as Egyptian and Roman.

from Bologna, our route goes on to Florence, but if you are making for the Adriatic coast, an extension through Ravenna is added at the end of this route

from Bologna S65 through Futa Pass (107 km) to Florence (Firenze)

This is a hard-driving route over mountains and round winding bends, taking over two hours compared with one hour on the motorway but well worth the effort for scenery and for catching the spirit of this part of Italy. You pass through the foothills of the Apennines then climb up to the Raticosa Pass, 968 m (3,175 ft), amid grand scenery which is rockier and more arid than Alpine passes of the north. But after the Futa Pass, you go downhill past walled towns, attractive villages, expensive old villas and castles. If you fork left at Pratolino, you come into Florence through Fiesole, an Etruscan and Roman city. From the terrace near the Monastery of St Francis you have a wonderful view of Florence. Or do it the easy way from café terraces in the cathedral square. Fiesole is 8 km from Florence, so you could hide here at night from the heat and crowds. Among visitors who did that were Shelley, Dickens, Anatole France and Lamartine.

Florence

Called an 'open-air museum', Florence has as many art treasures per square metre as anywhere in the world; it is nevertheless a bright, living city, and the only way around it is to park and walk. The traffic is appalling, the city is small enough for walking, and that way you will discover treasures that drivers would miss, like Benvenuto Cellini's masterpiece 'Perseus', showing Medusa's head, in the 14th-century Loggia dei Lanzi, once guardroom of foot soldiers.

As Florence has about 400 old palaces, more than 50 ancient churches, 22 interesting museums, and 5 charming parks, you will obviously not see it all, and the best thing to do is to pick from local guidebook the places most likely to interest you personally. But do leave some time to wander, to see the Florentine people going about their business and pleasure and to appreciate the remarkable light which has captivated artists through centuries and can turn even an austere, fortress-like palace built for defence like the Pitti into something of beauty.

Here follow the more obvious sights of Florence, the things you should not miss, in very brief form. I cannot hope to tell you all that you should see without writing a book on the city – and above all on its history and that of the Medicis.

Ponte Vecchio: 14th-century covered bridge with goldsmiths' and silversmiths' shops lining it; the only Florentine bridge not blown up by the Germans in 1944. Cynics say this shows German bad taste!

Mercato Nuovo: 16th-century covered straw-market; every sort of souvenir in straw and raffia from tablemats to handbags and sun hats. You are supposed to rub the nose of Porcellino, the bronze statue of a wild boar.

Uffizi Museum: in a Renaissance palace; one of the world's greatest; paintings by nearly all the great Italian and European masters from 13th to 18th centuries. One room devoted to Botticelli.

Pitti Palace: 15th century; later became seat of the Medicis. Paintings include eleven by Raphael, twelve by Rubens, also five by Veronese. Silver museum includes magnificent silverwork, porcelain, ivory, Limoges enamel, and tapestries. Royal apartments, open only Thursdays, Saturdays and alternate Sundays, have fine furnishings, ornaments and tapestries.

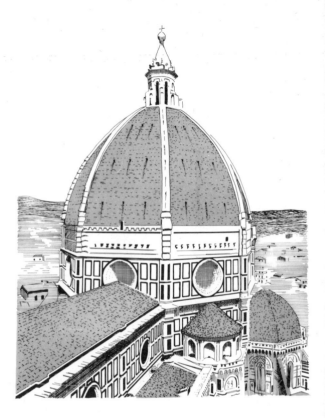

Florence
continued

Cathedral: begun 1296, finished 1434; its cupola bigger than that of St Peter's, Rome; sombre interior, but with superb frescos; 464 steps to the top of the dome for a superb view of Florence. Baptistry has beautiful mosaics; its bronze doors by Ghiberti were said by Michelangelo to be worthy to serve as the gates of paradise.

Boboli Gardens: attached to Pitti Palace; typically Italian, with terraces, statues, grottoes and fountains. Lovely views from top terrace.

Galleria del'Accademia: works of Michelangelo, including 'David', and 13th- to 16th-century Florentine paintings.

Bargello Palace: wonderful sculpture collection, including Cellini, Michelangelo, Donatello.

Palazzo Vecchio: 13th-century Medici palace until they moved to the Pitti; dreary outside, sumptuous décor inside, including frescos by Vasari and Michelangelo's 'Genius of Victory'.

Medici Chapels: tombs of Medicis designed by Michelangelo.

Casa Giudi, 8 piazza San Felice: home in Florence of Robert and Elizabeth Barrett Browning, English Victorian poets.

Restaurants and hotels
Trattoria Marione, via della Spada: used entirely by local workers. Cheap, absolutely typical, crowded, small. Meals about L5,000.

Ristorante Silvano, via del Prato: advertises cucina alla casalinga – home cooking. Away from centre; ordinary little restaurant used by local people. Meals L8,000-9,500. Good value.

Pensione Ariele, via Magenta: old villa away from crowds, almost opposite Opera House, only 10-minute walk from centre and reasonable parking prospects. Big old rooms with old furniture; small pretty garden; absolutely charming and quiet. Bed and breakfast (or half board also in summer season). Rooms L15,000-32,000. Limited accommodation, so telephone 211509.

Hotel Kraft, via Solferino: near Pensione Ariele and round corner from Opera House in quiet residential area but near river and 10-minute walk from city centre. Nicely modernized, comfortable hotel with most pleasant furnishings and a name for reliable cooking. Rooftop swimming pool, restaurant and sun terrace with views over Florence rooftops. Attentive service. A bit pricy but good value. Meals L13,500; rooms L40,000-65,000.

Jennings Riccioli, lungarno delle Grazie: overlooking river but nice front rooms with view can be noisy. Antique furnishings with modern plumbing; bed and breakfast L24,000-39,000.

Aprile, via della Scala: comfortable little hotel made from an old *palazzo.* Most friendly. No restaurant. Rooms L16,000-31,000.

Plaza Lucchesi, lungarno della Zecca Vecchia: excellent hotel in fine position on river Arno but dear, though very comfortable. Meals L18,000; closed Sundays; rooms L54,000-82,000.

Florence
continued

At Sesto Fiorentino (9 km) – Villa Villoresi, via delle Torri: delightful, in 13th-century villa, rated a first-class *pensione*, but four- to five-star rating with me. Run by Countess Villoresi, it has beautiful furniture and décor, enormous terrace overlooking swimming pool, children's pool and lovely grounds. Surprisingly reasonable but phone first for a room (tel. 4489032). Meals L12,000-15,000; closed Mondays; rooms with breakfast L25,000-40,000.

from Florence S222 through Greve to Castellina then left on S429 through Radda in Chianti to Siena by S408 (about 75 km)

Greve – Giovanni da Verazzano: small but food befitting good wine. Meals L9,000-16,000; rooms L8,000-15,000.

The real Chianti wine route, through hamlets and vine-covered hills. Beyond Grassina you cross Passo dei Pecorai, 300 m (1,100 ft) to Greve, nice little wine town. A short way down a road to the left is Castello di Uzzano, beautiful private residence of Count Castelbarco's family, an estate making excellent Chianti Classico, aged long in the wood.

Castellina – Villa Casalecchi: quiet country villa with pool. Beautiful décor, superb 'antique' bedrooms. Very good value. Half-*pensione* or full *pensione* (L46,000) only. Closed November-March.

Castellina has a 15th-century castle and town gate.

La Torre, piazza Umberto: truly excellent meals with fine Chianti. Try veal stewed in Chianti (stracotto di vitellone). Meals L10,000-12,000; closed Mondays.

Radda in Chianti – Albergo la Villa Miranda: another splendid country restaurant. Meals L10,000-12,000. Superb steak Fiorentina. In an old wine

Just south of Radda in Chianti is Meleto, where Barone Ricasoli makes some of his magnificent Brolio Chianti. But most is made at Castello di Brolio,

store; wine from its own vineyards.

which you can see by turning left a few kilometres further on. Here the family still lives. A hundred years ago Barone Ricasoli, prime minister of Italy, laid down the rules for making good Chianti from four grape types and made it one of the great and reliable wines of the world – so long as you get the genuine article. It is a snobbery that these great wines like Brolio are sold in ordinary bottles, not the straw-covered *fiasco*.

Siena

Siena has a few good, big expensive hotels on outskirts but those in the centre are mostly small and do not usually have

What a superb little city. Well worth studying a little of its history before you arrive. Its motto is: 'Siena opens its heart to you.'

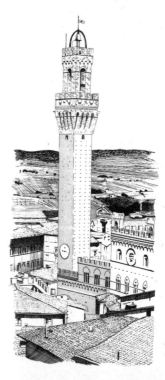

restaurants. This does not matter – there are plenty of good restaurants. Tourist office in the Campo will tell you which rooms are free.

La Toscana Albergo: simple, clean, has rooms with bath; charged me only L15,000 for a room. It has a garage.

Guido, vicolo Pier Pettinaio: my favourite; excellent meals for L15,000. Closed Mondays.

Nello La Taverna, via del Porione: almost on the Campo; warm atmosphere, unassuming; pleasant meals L9,000-13,000. Closed Mondays.

Grotta Santa Caterina da Bagoga, via della Galluza: old-style tavern with good ham, salami and grills; also serves Irish coffee. Meals around L8,000.

Roberto, just off via di Città: makes real pizza cooked in an open oven – excellent.

Alla Speranza, piazza del Campo: one of several around the Campo, this one is used by locals as well as outsiders. Good choice, good cooking, local Tuscan dishes. I had a 4-course meal for under L8,000, a good Chianti for L2,500.

Despite ancient history, old buildings down narrow old streets and round little squares, Siena is no museum piece. Its youth is eternal because of its old university with young students from round the world. They hurry to lectures down the streets, sit around squares putting the world right, and kiss in cafés and corners. Piazza del Campo, the great square which is nearer to heart-shape, surrounded by fine old palaces, shops and cafés of splendid harmony, is like a magnet. I can spend hours sitting beside the Fountain of Joy watching the light turning it from shadow to sunlight, watching the children, the old people, the students, the tourists, hurrying, dawdling, resting, idling.

Here the twice-yearly horse-race is held. The Palazzo Pubblico has a pretty inner courtyard and a belltower 95 m (286 ft) high with a good view from the top; a graceful 13th-century Gothic building made brighter by coats of arms on its windows. The cathedral of multicoloured marble, with a green and white marble belltower, is one of the nicest inside even in this area: superb 15th- to 16th-century paving, and mosaics depicting allegories, and sages such as Socrates and Dante. The picture gallery is rich in treasures, but the essence of Siena is in its old streets – via di Città and via Banchi di Sopra, the old houses which line them and the people who walk them.

In the old Medici fortress there is now a fine little wine museum and tasting centre in the cellars, open afternoons for the tasting of all the great and lesser wines of Tuscany.

Park and walk in Siena. Car park by the market.

S2 through San Quirico d'Orcia (for Pienza) 43 km, Ripa d'Orcia (5 km), Radiconfani (23 km), Acquapendente (3 km), Bolsena (32 km), Montefiascone (11 km),to Viterbo (917 km)

S2 to Rome (81 km)

See Fly-drive Tuscany route.

We are now following the same route as the Fly-drive Tuscany route but in the opposite direction. So Pienza, well worth the short diversion, is now to the *left* at San Quirico, 9 km along S146. You will drive *uphill* from Ripa d'Orcia to Radiconfani and then downhill from there through the Paglia valley.

Alternative route
Bologna to Rimini
(via Ravenna)

The direct motorway from Bologna to Rimini on the Adriatic coast is 112 km on A14. But a branch to Ravenna is worth taking.

Countryside and small towns are not exciting between Bologna and Ravenna, so take the motorway (74 km).

Ravenna is a great little city, with pleasant atmosphere and art treasures to lure most of us.

If you have seen only Roman mosaic floors you might think them interesting but not inspiring. The Byzantine Christian mosaics of Ravenna are in another world, and you do not have to be an art-lover or even a Christian to appreciate them. The depth, brightness of colour, clarity and form are incredible; almost unbelievable that they were made in the 5th and 6th- centuries. They look about ten years old, and surpass even the mosaics of Istanbul and Venice. No good trying to describe them – you must see them. Ravenna still keeps the art alive in its School of Mosaicists. How this old art form would enliven some of our hotels and public buildings!

Main mosaics are in St Vitalis church, Galla Placidia tomb, Neoni Baptistry, Basilica of St Apollinaris the New (an impressive building where the wall and ceiling mosaics appeal most to the layman), and the other Basilica of St Apollinaris in Classe, 5 km south on S16. Not just beautiful patterns, but depicting people and scenes.

Worth seeing, too, is Ravenna's Giardino Pubblico (public gardens) with a fine loggia (1508), the poet

Dante's tomb (1321), and the charming main square, piazza del Popolo, with Venetian columns (1483).

Ravenna is a happy little city, especially when students fill the streets and cafés early each evening. Italian students have a way of bringing their old cities alive.

Restaurants and hotels
With the coast so near, you may not want to stay overnight, but if you do, a useful, quiet little hotel, in an old merchant's house, is Argentario, via Roma 45: comfortable, not luxurious; no restaurant; rooms L15,000-25,000.

Bella Venezia, via 4 Novembre: perhaps the best restaurant; meals L11,000-15,000; closed Mondays.

At Marina di Ravenna, 13 km, not a very good resort – Maddalena, viale delle Nazioni: really excellent fish restaurant; meals L10,000-14,000; closed Mondays; rooms L10,000-17,000; open April to November.

From Ravenna, S16 along coast to Rimini (52 km).

Route 3
Brenner Pass to Venice
(from Innsbruck)

A route for those who want to see something of the Austrian Tyrol on their way to Italy – a mountain-lovers' road. The journey across Germany can be very fast on motorways. Or you could come through Zürich and join at Bolzano if it is Switzerland you want to see first.

Once again, there is superb scenery on this route, and in places we have given the alternative of slower, winding but rewarding roads or more direct roads. The dullest stretch is for a short distance before Bassano. Asolo is so attractive that you might want to spend a night or two there.

The Bolzano–Trento area was part of the Hapsburg Austro-Hungarian Empire until the Treaty of Versailles in 1919, so its food and the very names of its dishes are a mixture of Italian and Austrian. You may find on a menu wurstel con crauti, which is the Italian version of wurst mit kraut, sausage with sauerkraut. Strudel is the favourite sweet, local gnocchi are called canederli, a corruption of Austrian knödel, and have the same dumpling touch, being made with flour, breadcrumbs, ham and sausage. Small ravioli, stuffed with meat, vegetables and cream cheese, are called either ravioletti or schulpfkrapfeln!

It is all good mountain food, and the combination of Austrian weight and Italian subtlety works well. As in the Veneto further south, most cooking is with butter, and rice is more popular than pasta.

There are very good, if not great, wines – strong red Santa Maddelena loved in Austria; Merlot Trentino, a fine dry red for meals; Italian white Riesling, usually drier than when made with the German grape; Terlano white, heavier than most Italian white wines. Lagrein Rosato is a sparkling rosé from Bolzano.

In the Veneto hills, as in Venice, you find good risotto, but usually with meat instead of Venetian fish. Treviso has risi con la luganega (rice with highly spiced sausage). Venice has a nice mutton risotto (risotto in Cavroman), but the fish risotto there can be delicious. My favourite is with mussels – di cozze. Another Venetian delicacy is pesce in savor (fried fish marinated in vinegar, onion and spices). The excellent fegato alla Veneziana uses oil for cooking the liver.

Around Asolo and Treviso you can get good game, local trout, and excellent chicken and sausages. In Venice I would make for fish restaurants, preferably those showing the fish on a slab in a display case, and eat it fresh-grilled.

Venice gets its ordinary wines from the Veneto hills north and south of Treviso. They are reliable. But, of course, westward are some splendid wines – the red Bardolino and Valpolicella, Soave white and the dry Tocai, unrelated to sweet Tokay of Hungary. Route 4 passes through their growing areas, so you will find more about them there.

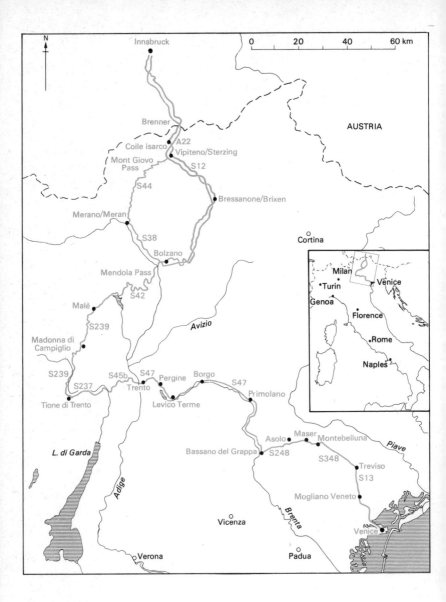

Route 3
Brenner Pass to Venice
(from Innsbruck)

Coming down from Innsbruck to Brenner, then from Brenner, you have a choice of three ways: motorway to Bolzano, S12 through Bressanoné (Brixen), or the spectacular, beautiful, harder-driving route through Merano which I recommend after snow has gone

or finally into Italy at Colle Isarco, then S12 to Vipiteno, S44 to Merano by Mont Giovo Pass (good road but many hairpins); usually closed November to early June, during which time I recommend the motorway; highest point 2,200 m (6,900 ft), down to 320 m (1,000 ft) at Merano. A few narrowish bits – 3.3 m (13 ft)

Merano – Andrea, via Galilei: Andrea Hellrigl's restaurant is probably the best in the Bolzano area, is starred by *Michelin* and praised by *Guida d'Italia*, so is not cheap and gets full (ring Merano 24400). Among many fine dishes I loved especially filetti di trota alla griglia, small trout split open, sauté in butter with bay leaf and onions, and served in a cream sauce with white mushrooms called porcini. Superb. Good wines from a fairly good wine area, Alto Adige. Meals L15,000-20,000. Closed Wednesdays.

Meraner Weinkost, corso della Libertà: country décor; for tasting local wines and

Spa, centre of fruit area, with fine scenery, it has cable cars and chair-lifts for winter sports, summer views and walking. Famous for its roses, which smell sweet, look beautiful and last long, and for grapes. Modern spa centre for taking the waters and an old grape cure for obesity – gradually cutting out all food except grapes, which is claimed to help fat people get thin and the Twiggies put on curves. Alas, you are supposed to eat the grapes, not drink their juice. Typical old Tyrolean town, with old and picturesque buildings in centre and Austrian Empire 'grand hotel' style surrounding them. Hot in midsummer.

Merano
continued

food, including mountain sausage and cheese; meals L8,000-13,000. Closed mid-day and Sundays. Open till 2.30 a.m.

Terlaner Weinstuber Putz, via Portici: real old local restaurant with typical local cooking of the South Tyrol–Alto Adige style as befits a place which politicians have called both Austrian and Italian according to who won the previous war. Cheap, full meal with choice for L9,000, menu for L7,000. Closed Wednesdays.

Anatol, via Castagni: good quiet overnight hotel with baths in every room. Meals L7,000; bed and breakfast L16,000-23,000 per person. Garden; pool. Open March-November.

Castel Tirolo (5km north) is 12th-century castle of medieval counts of Tyrol. Carved doorways, two-tier Romanesque chapel with 14th-century frescos, also throne room with knights' hall.

S38 through Terlano to Bolzano (29 km)

Terlano – Weingarten: quiet with shaded garden. Heated swimming pool. Meals L6,500-10,000; bed and breakfast L9,000-14,500 per person. Open March-November.

Bolzano – good choice of restaurants.

Da Abramo, piazza Gries, near corso Libertà: local favourite, unpretentious but recently renovated; Italian cooking, including fine spaghetti and a risotto alle lumache (with snails).

Terlano is known for its white wine made from classic grapes such as Sauvignon, Italian Riesling, Traminer and Pinot Blanc (called Terlaner here) growing on steep hillsides.

Bolzano is industrial and commercial but has some nice buildings, including the 14th-century Franciscan church, with cloisters and gardens; nearby 13th-century Castle Roncolo (2 km north) is perched high on a rock; has

Meals L10,000-18,000. Closed Sunday evenings, Mondays and mid-July to mid-August.

Caterpillar, via Castel Flavon: excellent cooking, especially fish, which includes not only mountain and lake fish but seafood. Outstanding mixed grill of fish usually includes salmon and scampi; meat grills are good, too. Choice of 100 Italian wines. Meals L10,000-18,000.

Hotel Grifone, piazza Walther: central and thoroughly recommended, but not cheap. Pool, gardens, comfortable rooms; very good meals with local or national Italian cooking; everything seems good, from local sausage to roast veal with asparagus and good fish and desserts. Also Lago di Caldaro wines from west of Bolzano – clear garnet when young, brick-red when three years old, subtle taste and sold extensively in Austria and Germany under the Germanic name for the lake – Kalterersee. Meals L15,000-20,000; rooms L35,000-55,000. Closed Sundays and November-March.

Hotel Herzog, piazza del Grano: no restaurant but comfortable for overnights at moderate prices. Rooms L15,000-27,000. Closed January and February.

frescos of chivalrous legends such as Tristan's story. Worth a visit.

Santa Maddalena, on a mountain 2 km east, produces the good red wine drunk extensively in the Dolomites and in Austria; soft, velvety red wine made from local Schiava grapes, mature after two years and splendid with roasts, game, sausage or cheese.

from Bolzano, retrace S38 northwards for 3 km, then left on to S42 through Mendola Pass (usually open, road wide enough for caravans, good surface but winding), through Male, then S239 to left (winding road) to Madonna di Campiglio; still on S239 through Rendena valley to Tione di Trento

then S237 past Lake Toblino and on to S45b to Trento (about 160 km)

At Madonna di Campiglio most hotels have two seasons, winter (usually December to end of April) and summer (July to mid-September), so you may have difficulty finding one in other months.

Hotel Touring: (open as above) good value. Meals L8,000-10,000; rooms L15,000-35,000.

Fairly hard driving but magnificent scenery. The easier and quicker way is to take S12, which runs parallel to the motorway to A22 (distance Bolzano to Trento 57 km).

A small mountain resort among fir trees. Splendid views, especially from Monte Spinale (five minutes by cable car). Lake Toblino, fringed by rushes, has a small old castle on a peninsula.

Trento is Trent, where the Catholic council sat 1545–63 laying down canons of faith to fight the

Trento – Grand Hotel Trento and Rist. al Caminetto, via Alfieri: nice position opposite park with summer terrace; restaurant serves true local dishes with fresh meat, dairy products and vegetables from the hill pastures; good value, lots of gnocchi, local dumplings, game and strudel. Meals L13,000; rooms L26,000-41,000. Restaurant closed Sundays.

Chiesa, via San Marco: in 16th-century villa, excellent value, unusual dishes. Will serve a complete meal using apples in many ways; also tagliatelle pasta with walnuts (splendid), cheese strudel, mountain trout, lake salmon trout. Meals L13,000-17,000. Closed Sunday evenings, Mondays and last fortnight in June. Sergio Chiesa is a national award-winning chef.

Nino, via Travai: very good trattoria with variety of dishes at lowish prices.

spread of Protestantism – the Counter-Reformation. Trento is on the Adige river and surrounded by rocky heights leading down to hill pastures and valleys. Still retains some Austrian influence from the Hapsburg Empire. The majestic Romanesque cathedral, where the council met, is in a pleasant square surrounding a lively fountain of Neptune and including Rella houses with 15th-century frescos. The cathedral has a rose window depicting the wheel of fortune.

The Castle of Good Counsel (Buon Consiglio), residence of the bishops and now a museum, is most interesting and has some fine frescos and impressive courts. Trento is an elegant mountain town.

S47 to Pergine, Levico, Borgo, Primolano, to Bassano del Grappa (88 km)

Levico – Bellavista: comfortable hotel with garden; well furnished. Pool. Meals L10,000-17,000; rooms L20,000-34,000. Open only May-September and one month from 20 December.

Levico Terme is a tiny spa with health-bringing mountain air and strong mineral waters. In a bowl of hills beside a little lake, it has a backcloth of vineyards, orchards and woods and some 16th-century houses in town. A restful place.

Bassano del Grappa

Bassano – Al Sole da Tiziano, via Vittorelli: very good restaurant offering local specialities according to season, such as the local white asparagus in April and May, spit-roast duck (July-April), local fungi dishes (September-December), and guinea fowl. Meals L10,000-14,000.

Cà 7, 1.5 km north on S47: in a 17th-century-style Venetian villa, good meals but pricy at L18,000-25,000.

Bassano is a pleasant little city on the banks of the Brenta, below Monte Grappa, a mountain of 1,800 m (5,800 ft) revered by Italians for the heroic defence here by Italian armies against Austrians in 1917-18. Bassano itself is delightful – narrow streets and squares with arcades and houses painted Venetian style; its originally 13th-century covered bridge, rebuilt several times since, has become a sort of national symbol of revival – a phoenix. Nice views from it and it leads to a 13th-century church. A place for wandering the streets. They make pottery and very good grappa – the rather fiery brandy made from grape husks.

S248 then small turning left to Asolo, (16 km)

S248 then lane left to Maser

See Fly-drive Venice route.

Do not miss either Asolo, delightful town with superb views, where Robert Browning lived; or the magnificent Palladio villa at Maser with Veronese frescos – one of the great houses of Europe – see Fly-drive Venice for opening days.

S248 to
Montebelluna,
then S348 to
Treviso (35 km)

This area is known for some unusual gastronomic treats, like the red lettuce of Treviso, with purplish leaves and white stalk, and the multicoloured variegated lettuce of Castelfranco; huge crayfish from San Polo di Piave (north-east) and a famous sausage called juganega.

Treviso – Al Fogher, viale della Repubblica: medium-priced comfortable hotel on outskirts with very good restaurant. Rooms L11,000-21,000.

Alfredo El Toula, via Colato 26: Alfredo Beltrame has one of the best restaurants in the Veneto, comparable with some of the best in Venice for its cooking. Most dishes are his own

Treviso is picturesque and interesting, with 15th-century ramparts and canals intersecting it. Little alleys behind the attractive piazza dei Signori cross the canals in which waterwheels turn. Churches rich in frescos; many houses, too, painted with frescos Venetian style, and streets are arcaded. Market days in the old part

Treviso
continued

creations so the names do not mean much, but do try blinis al brie (a sort of cheese crêpe), lovely risotto in many forms, and splendid cockerel (galleto) with herbs. Put yourself in his hands. You can get a full meal for L14,000, but L18,000-20,000 is more likely. Closed Monday and early August.

Beccherie, piazza Ancillotto 10: nearer to my pocket than Alfredo. Happy, enthusiastic management serving good meals, excellent value. Venetian emphasis on rice. Meals L10,000-12,000.

of town are Tuesdays and Saturdays. A delightful little place. Walk along ramparts to north of town and see the Alps.

S13 to Venice (30 km) via Mogliano Veneto (18 km)

Zerman, near Mogliano – Hotel Villa Condulmer: strictly for the lucky people with money to spend. One of my favourite hotels in Europe, although I cannot afford it any more. Mind you, you would pay at least double for anything comparable in Rome, Venice or Florence. Meals L16,000-30,000; rooms L22,000-50,000. Closed mid-Nov. to 28 Feb.

You stay in a beautiful villa in a lovely park, magnificent decorations, including 18th-century frescos, lovely period furniture, and the feeling that you are guest of the old Venetian family of Condulmer who, in the generation which built this villa, produced a victorious general, a leading politician and a pope.

Route 4
Mont Blanc tunnel/
Great St Bernard
to Venice
(via Milan)

The classic old route to Venice, now superseded by
the motorway A4. It runs parallel to A4 from Milan,
but there are so many fine places and things to see
that if you took the motorway you would be driving
off it every few miles in order not to miss some of
Italy's greatest treasures.

Although Lake Garda is more beautiful towards the
top – see Fly-drive Venice route – it is interesting here
at the bottom and you can catch boats to explore the
lake.

Verona is a priceless city – one of the pleasant
surprises of life. Vicenza, little known to Britons, is a
gem. Padua is bigger, so it takes time to find its
treasures, but they are worth seeking.

Unless you are in a great hurry to get to Venice, take
a boat from Villa Nazionale at Strà along the Brenta
canal, past magnificent villas built for patricians of
Venice in the 17th and 18th centuries by some of
history's greatest architects. They were rowed in
luxury to the tunes of musicians. The new boat uses
an engine, music is taped, but it is comfortable and
has a bar. You return to Strà by coach to pick up your
car. Check times of boats in Padua at CIT, piazza
Cavour (telephone 25349).

A good route for food, even better for wine. You start
with the mountain food of Aosta, with a French bias,
and the varied dishes of Piedmont – see Route 1.

Milan is proud of its cuisine. Saffron is used freely.
Rice is popular, too, so you get risotto Milanese (rice
cooked in chicken broth with saffron and butter, so

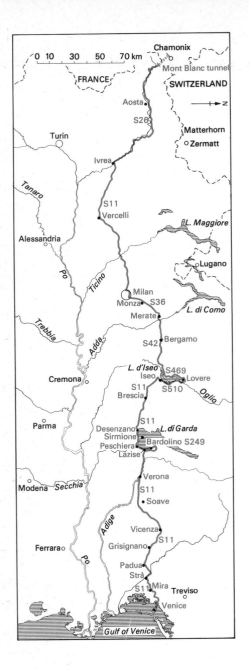

that it is creamy, like a savoury rice pudding, served with grated cheese). Osso buco alla Milanese is world famous – shinbone of veal with meat intact, stewed with white wine and tomato and served with risotto. But the best-known dish is costeletta alla Milanese – a simple veal cutlet coated with egg and breadcrumbs and fried in butter. Milan minestrone soup uses rice, not pasta. Lombardy is a land of cheeses, including bel paese, gorgonzola (served soft, not from the fridge!) and soft creamy stracchino.

The western end of the Veneto, including Verona and area, owes much of its cuisine to Parma and Bologna, although it would never admit it. The result is excellent – good creamy pasta as well as excellent rice dishes, fish but also good meat and meat sauces. Vicenza has some good turkey recipes and also marsoni, small fish from the local river. Verona, where cooking is usually good, has an odd soup called risi e bisi – very thick, made of rice and peas flavoured with chopped celery, onion and ham.

You pass the vineyards of Bardolino and Soave on this route, skirt those producing Valpolicella. I have written of them in the route text. The Italians like Valpolicella young. It is subtler that way. But if you like a strong and solid red wine with your meat, try the Classico Valpolicella five or six years old. You will know that you have had a drink.

Verona's Recioto is a likable sweet dessert wine – made from grapes dried in ventilated lofts.

Lombardy wines are little known outside Italy, but some are fine. Try Inferno or Sassella – but not when young. They should be at least three years old, preferably five. They are deep ruby red, warming, and go well with roasts, game or sausage dishes.

Even the good wines on this route are reasonably priced.

Route 4
Mont Blanc tunnel/
Great St Bernard
to Venice
(via Milan)

Mont Blanc
tunnel through
Aosta and Ivrea
to Vercelli (S26d,
S26, S11)

See Route 1.

S11
Milan (Milano)
(74 km)

Milan is a small city surrounded by a vast web of
industrial and residential suburbs which,
paradoxically, make it the second biggest city in Italy.
As with all big cities, there is far too much to see in a
short stay and it is best to consult a
fairly lengthy guidebook to the city
and pick what interests you. But
do start with the cathedral, which
would impress even a visitor in
Milan only to watch a football
match. In white marble, it has
135 spires, 2,200 sculptures
decorating its outside and
another 2,000 inside. It was
started in 1386 and finished
in 1809 by order of
Napoleon. Although the
inside, being bare, looks
severe it is most
impressive, with five huge
aisles. Go to the roof by
lift (250 lire) to see the
remarkable detail of the
building.

Vittorio Emanuele Gallery: a covered way with expensive and interesting shops and a pleasant if pricy café joins the cathedral to La Scala, the great opera house (open daily except in August). Other beautiful and expensive shops are along corso Vittorio Emanuele and corso Venezia. Night life is mainly around piazza Santa Babila.

Of the usual tourist sites, the impressive old castle of the Sforza family is worth seeing and has a fine art gallery. Alongside is the beautiful Sempione Park, with sports arena and aquarium. The Poldi-Pezzoli Museum in via Manzoni is a beautifully furnished nobleman's villa with exquisite art treasures, mainly Renaissance to 17th century – including Botticelli's 'Madonna' and Giovanni Bellini's 'Pietà' (closed Mondays).

Useful if pricy car parks around cathedral include one high-rise, one underground. The fainthearted, like me, park near their hotels and use the underground (MM – Metropolitana Milanese).

If you have the right car and fancy playing at being a Grand Prix driver for one memorable lap, take road S36 (11 km on way to Bergamo) to Monza Autodromo, Italian Grand Prix circuit with long fast straights and seven corners. Drive round for 200 lire (300 on Sundays). Grand Prix drivers reach over 175 m.p.h., which is not advisable for amateurs! There are also two golf courses, a swimming pool in the same park (Villa Reale), with beautiful landscaped gardens in the English manner and a neoclassical, formerly royal, villa.

Restaurants and hotels
Most hotels, especially those moderately priced, and many little restaurants are around the huge 'Mussolini Gothic' central railway station, on which Il Duce had the inevitable balcony built from which he could harangue the crowds in the square. Restaurant competition is fierce, and by studying menus outside you can find good-value meals.

Taverna Gran Sasso, piazzale Principessa Clotilde: set meal of seven courses, wine and liqueur. Boisterous, crowded, informal; wooden tables; Abruzzi cooking. Meals with drinks L16,000. Closed Sundays and July.

Restaurant Gran San Bernardo, via Borgese: well known, thoroughly deserves its *Michelin* star; popular, so book ahead (telephone 389000). Real Milanese dishes, including risotto alla Milanese (rice cooked in chicken broth, flavoured with saffron, served with butter and grated cheese to give it a creamy effect, like a rich savoury rice pudding), costoletta alla Milanese (veal cutlet coated with egg and breadcrumbs, fried in butter) and, above all, cazzoeula (classic Lombardy stew of pork, sausages, carrots, cabbage, white wine, with polenta maize bread); also foiolo (tripe with garlic, onions, mushrooms, tomatoes and white wine – dish of Milan's workers promoted to the gourmet class). Owner-chef Alfredo Valli. Meals L13,000-20,000. Closed Sundays, early August and Christmas holidays.

Giordano, via Torti, corso Genova: not Milanese but Emilia Romagna cuisine from Bologna, capital of Italian cooking. Good service, excellent food. Meals L11,000-16,000. Closed Mondays and part of August.

Al Grissino, via Tiepolo: simple restaurant used by locals for good cooking and excellent antipasto (starters). Meals around L10,000-15,000. Closed Wednesdays.

Giardino, Alzaia Naviglio Grande (near river Naviglio): colourful little inn in old courtyard, with tables under trees outside in summer and entertainment by passing musicians. Excellent food. Fairly cheap. Closed Tuesdays.

Hotel de la Ville, via Hoepli: comfortable and reasonably priced for a first-class hotel: conveniently placed between cathedral and La Scala. Meals L14,000; rooms L53,000-65,000.

Lord Internazionale Hotel, via Spadari: despite its name, a simple, cheapish hotel with small rooms but clean and plenty of character. No restaurant. Rooms L28,000-42,000.

Antica Locanda Solferino, via Castelfidardo: delightful old tavern with 1890s décor and furnishings; in old Brera area near La Scala. Simple, cheap, but popular, so check by telephone. Rooms L20,000-22,000. Closed August.

Scoffona wine house, via Victor Hugo: good snacks with wine from all Italy. You stand up.

S36 to Monza and Merate, then local road to right to Bergamo (49 km)

Ristorante La Vendemmia, via Fara: expensive, but fine cooking in delightful atmosphere of a 17th-century house or its garden. Local dishes such as smoked goose breast, salami and smoked hams, and pancakes made from the local soft creamy cheese, telaggio. Meals L15,000-25,000. Closed Wednesdays.

Bergamo: split-level city up a hillside. Lower half town-planned by Mussolini's favourite architect, Piacentini, the upper half a quiet, charming old town little known to Britons but well worth visiting. In lower part, Città Bassa, Accademia Carrara has fine old furniture and pictures by Rubens and Van Dyck. Funicular to upper city, Città

Bergamo *continued*	Hotel del Moro, large Porta Nuova: simple hotel with good restaurant: good fish antipasto, or smoked wild boar; excellent spaghetti, cannelloni and gnocchi; risotto with gorgonzola cheese, good grilled fish and meat; wines from several countries. Meals L12,000-17,000. Closed Wednesdays; rooms L15,000-25,000. Closed early August.	Alta, which has lovely medieval buildings within medieval walls; palaces in styles ranging from 12th to 16th centuries Palladian style. See especially piazza Vecchia.
S42, then S469 to Lovere (41 km)		After some industry, the road reaches the shores of Lake d'Iseo, 24 km (15 miles) long by 8 km (5 miles) wide, almost surrounded by mountains and one lake which few tourists except Italians know. Vineyards on its shores and a big island, Monte Isola. West side is in Bergamo province, east side in Brescia. Lovere is partly industrial; Iseo (in Brescia) is a resort.
S510 to Iseo and Brescia (62 km)		Brescia is pleasant but essentially industrial; piazza della Loggia is Renaissance, showing the Venetian influence in Brescia's history.
S11 Desenzano (31 km)	Park Hotel: comfortable, lake views; good value. I have not eaten here. Meals L10,000-12,000; closed Thursdays; rooms L18,000-26,000.	Charming fishing town and holiday resort on Lake Garda; photogenic old port, old castle, Roman mosaics in Villa Romana, 'Last Supper' by Tiepolo in parish

Hotel Vittorio, Porto Vecchio: old hotel with rooms overlooking tiny old port and the lake; old-fashioned rooms but pleasant atmosphere and fair meals, including trout and carp from lake. Meals L8,000-14,000; closed Mondays; rooms L12,000-18,000.

Rustic Locanda, via Castello: simple trattoria in side street; very clean; cheap good food; service patchy. Meals L7,500-12,000.

Tripoli, piazza Matteoti: clean, pleasant *albergo* on promenade; front rooms good, back rooms comfortable but view of walls. All with WC/shower. Meals L7,000-10,000; rooms L14,000-22,000.

church; but mostly a place to relax overnight or longer, take a short boat trip and eat. Our grandfathers stayed here. Crowded high season.

Lake Garda is largest of Italian lakes.

S11, then local road left to Sirmione (9 km)

Plenty of hotels of all grades. Villa Cortine, via Grotte: in lakeside gardens; lovely but dear. Meals L20,000; rooms L35,000-65,000. Open April-October.

Grifone da Luciano, via delle Bisse: nice garden and terrace with lake views; meals are very good value; try a very tasty cannelloni and lake fish; open April-October; restaurant closed Wednesdays. Meals L8,000-14,000; rooms (simple) L14,000-19,000.

On a tongue of land sticking into the lake; Romans built villas. Catullus was born here and the ruins of a villa and the local caves are named after him. See also castle of the Scala family and lovely views of lake. Spa with natural hot waters for baths and inhaling.

S11 to Peschiera
(8 km) then S249
Bardolino 'wine
road' to left
alongside Lake
Garda to Lazise
and Bardolino
(12 km)

At Bardolino – Aurora, via San Severo: very ordinary to look at, but serves good local country dishes, including stuffed trout from the lake, salmon trout and nice local veal dishes. Good place to compare the Bardolino and Valpolicella wines. Meals L10,500-18,000. Closed Mondays and November to 20 December.

Lazise is small fishing port with medieval castle, once belonging to Scaliger family which ruled Verona. Shore here is uninteresting but the wine is interesting enough – light, refreshing, to be drunk young and cold if you like young, cold red wine (it gives me indigestion – even the new Beaujolais!). Drink the Classico – better than ordinary Bardolino from near the S11 road. Just east, towards Verona, is the rival Valpolicella Classico country – a slightly heavier wine, almost cherry coloured, which the Italians like to drink young, putting it straight into the bottles, not wooden casks, to stop it ageing. They export it when older.

S249 back to
Lazise, then
local road left
to Verona
(about 20 km)

Verona is a truly beautiful and colourful city, with dark red bricks, white stone, whiter marble and deep-green cypresses, making a pattern of Roman, medieval and Renaissance architecture which seem to harmonize after so many centuries.

Start in piazza Bra, one of the most impressive squares in the world, with fountains, pavement restaurants and cafés, buildings of many centuries, but all dominated by the grandiose Roman arena of the 1st century, second biggest Roman amphitheatre to Rome's Coliseum – 152 m (500 ft) long, 128 m (420 ft) wide, 30 m (100 ft) high. It could hold 25,000 spectators, and still does in August when opera and concerts are performed in its bowl, said to have perfect acoustics. Horse fair held here in March brings farmers from all over Italy and resembles the prototype of the American state

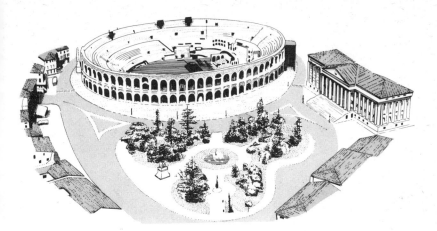

fairs. Main street, via Mazzini, leads off Bra past fine shops to piazza delle Erbe, the old Roman forum round which chariot races used to be run and which is now a flower, fruit and vegetable market, with stalls which have been joined by others selling cheap tourist souvenirs. Renaissance palaces, with pink marble columns, and old houses surround the square and in the via Cappello at number 23, just off the square, Juliet Capulet *(Romeo and Juliet)* is supposed to have lived. There is a suitable balcony and a statue to her. Her family, Dal Cappello, lived in this district and the marble coat of arms over the archway has a hat *(cappello)* which was the seal of the family. I hope that she lived there – it is such a pretty house, even if sceptics claim it was really an inn called Dal Cappello.

Almost next to Erbe is piazza dei Signori, with buildings from the 12th century onwards around it and Dante's statue in the middle. A lovely elegant square. Verona has an embarrassing wealth of treasures for people with limited time, but I would not miss the ornate tombs of the Scaliger family (the ruling Scalas), Juliet's tomb, the magnificent bridge and castle of the Scala family, and among many lovely churches, the church of Santa Anastasia (13th to 15th centuries) with some magnificent frescos and terracottas, especially Pisanello's 'St George and the Princess'. Though very much a tourist town, Verona remains delightful and an absolute Mecca of art and beauty.

Superb views of the city from Castel San Pietro. See also Giusti Palace Gardens; laid out 1580 and terraced in the Italian manner.

Restaurants and hotels
Pedavena, piazza Bra: possibly the best, and dearest, of restaurants around piazza Bra; excellent antipasto including outstanding raw ham; try also crêpe schiaccianoci (fettuccine, the Roman-style tagliatelle pasta, with mushrooms), and good meat dishes. Meals L12,000-20,000. Closed Mondays.

Torcoloti, via Zambelli: quiet, sedate, good; though the food is not entirely 'local' it is excellent and the service most friendly; excellent gnocchi paste verde (flavoured with spinach) with gorgonzola sauce; good steak and excellent salads and vegetables. Meals L9,000-12,000. Closed Sundays and Monday evenings.

Due Mori, vicoletto Due Mori, opposite Santa Anastasia church (*not* Due *Torri):* friendly, a touch of old Italy; moderately priced. Menu L8,500.

Many restaurants in streets fanning off piazza Bra, especially north-east towards via Zambelli and south off corso Porta Nuova. One of the cheapest is off Porta Nuova in via dei Mutilati, called Trattoria Big Ben with meals at L5,000-8,000.

Al Bragozzo, via del Pontiere: excellent fish restaurant; try fish and shellfish antipasto; spiedino misto mare (with a beautiful shellfish sauce); pesce a cartoccio (fish baked in a paper case to keep all its flavour); good local wines: Soave, Valpolicella, Bardolino. Closed Mondays.

Bar Pizzeria Cavour, piazza Bra, serves excellent freshly made pizza and good lasagne. Pizza costs L2,000-3,000 for a large one, pasta dishes about

L1,200. Service not sophisticated, but passing scene interesting.

Many hotels of all grades. Useful for simple overnights are: San Luca, galleria Volto San Luca: near piazza Bra; no restaurant but a garage; rooms L22,000–35,000.

Verona, corso Porto Nuova; simple but most rooms with baths. Rooms L15,000–22,000.

Accademia, via Scala: pleasant, modern furnishings, nice restaurant; parking problems, but garage near by. Meals L12,000–17,000; closed Sunday evenings and Wednesdays; rooms L30,000–45,000.

Bologna, piazzetta Scalette Rubiani: useful hotel close to piazza Bra and Arena. Comfortable, adequate rooms. Meals L10,000; rooms L20,000–28,000.

S11
to Soave
(on small road
to left)
(25 km)

Roxi, piazza Castagneti: modern, with an uninviting name, it serves good pasta, local meat, vegetables and fruit, cooked in Venetian and Veronese manner. Soave wine, of course. Meals L8,000–11,000. Closed Mondays and late August.

Castle and ramparts of the Scaligers (14th century) and photogenic walled town whose name should be on any self-respecting wine list. Though once a lot of mediocre wines were labelled Soave, the real thing is refreshing and can be drunk young and fresh or three or more years old when it is softer and rather bland. Classico is stronger and better.

Basilica da Carlo, via Teso, piazza Erbe: in the vegetable market; my favourite; modern but with right atmosphere. Clean rooms, excellent food with local dishes such as baccalà Vicentina (salt cod tasting better than it sounds), duck with bigoli (a form of spaghetti), veal with seafood cream sauce, fresh vegetables from market outside, fine antipasto, including a country-smoked ham from Veneto hills and asparagus from Bassano. Soft cheese of Asiago, seasoned cheese Vezzena. Prices have risen. Meals L8,500-12,000; rooms L25,000-35,000. Parking difficult after 7.00 a.m. when market opens!

Jolly Campo Marzio, viale Roma: one of the Jolly chain of hotels for businessmen – clean, comfortable, medium prices; convenient – beside the park, 1 km from city centre, own parking. Efficient service. I have not eaten here, but local businessmen do. Meals L12,000; rooms L28,500-45,000.

Al Pozzo da Sergio, via San Antonio: some unusual dishes, plus a good pizzeria and fine roasts such as leg of pork. Try excellent mushroom soup, bigoli alla baccalà (spaghetti with fish sauce), cutlets of pork,

A gem of a city, adored by architects and lovers of Renaissance buildings but not much known to British tourists. Palladio worked and died here – the stonemason who studied the buildings of ancient Rome and revolutionized architecture in the 16th century, changing its direction not only in Italy but in England, France and Russia. Inigo Jones was his admirer. His style influenced even the White House in Washington, and London's National Gallery. His home city is naturally rich in his work and a young architect trying to break away from modern concrete filing-cabinet architecture should spend time in Vicenza and around the Veneto. You must park and walk.

Most of its treasures are external. The narrow main street, corso Andrea Palladio, is lined with houses designed by him or his pupils and you need to cross and recross the busy traffic to see them. Delightful old streets lead off it to piazza dei Signori, the big main square.

Palladio designed the impressive basilica, where the local nobles used to meet, and the Loggio del Capitano, the governor's palace; the clocktower is

and very good desserts.
Courteous service. Meals
L10,000–14,000. Closed
Wednesdays.

Due Mori, via Due Ruote
(tiny road off corso
Palladio): popular but small;
old style; tourist menu at
L6,500; also a pizzeria; à la
carte meals around
L10,000.

12th century; Monte di
Pietà, adorned with frescos
and framing the little
baroque church of St
Vincent, is 15th and 16th
century.

Down steps beside the
basilica is the animated and
interesting fruit and
vegetable market, with
narrow back streets. This is
a town for wandering.
There's the Salvi garden
with two little waterways,

the courtyard of the bishop's palace opposite the cathedral, and the museum with a fine collection of Venetian paintings, a Jan Breughel and a Van Dyck.

Teatro Olimpico is remarkable. Designed by Palladio on the plan of a Greek theatre, he left it uncompleted on his death. But another great designer, Scamozzi, finished it. It was the first covered theatre in Europe. The stage sets are permanent; they show Thebes' streets in ancient Greece with a remarkable three-dimensional appearance. They were built for the first performance of Sophocles' *Oedipus Rex*. The scenery must inhibit modern producers, who therefore stick to the classical plays. Quite a challenge here for some writer like Dennis Potter to combine his own talents with that scenery!

Take the Este road south-east and second turning right for Villa Capra – called the Rotunda – Palladio's best-known villa, extensively 'borrowed' by British architects, in particular. You can enter the grounds, not the building, on Tuesdays, Thursdays and Saturdays.

Padua – Dotto, via Squarcione: best for local dishes, which include several with tripe, bean soup and noodles, and a lot of rice, including risotto with quails. Also pappardelle, a flat pasta, served with game-bird sauce. Meals L10,000–15,000. Closed Sunday evenings, Mondays and August.

La Padovenelle at Ponte di Brenta, 6 km along S11 towards Venice, at the race track: elegant, pricy hotel with fine food. Venetian and international cuisine. Good wine list. Meals L12,000–20,000; rooms L30,000–60,000. Restaurant closed Sunday evenings, Mondays and first three weeks of August.

For an unusual snack in Padua late afternoon onwards try Ostricaro, via Marsilio: serves succulent fresh mussels with white wine.

Grisignano is along a little road to the right, in early summer rich in roses. Another little road from here to the river Bacchiglione reaches village of Montegaldo, with the castle Grimani Marcello. A storybook castle, on a hill, forbidding from outside, delightful inside, with remarkable frescos (grotesque in the dining-room, amusing in the bathroom), interesting chapel, music-room, fascinating armoury. Don't walk the rampart if you have vertigo. Check opening times at Vicenza – confusion at time of writing.

Padua – perhaps because it has no Romeo and Juliet, the city is less known to Britons than Verona, and this valley of the Po can have miserable foggy days in winter. It has been called the 'city of the café without doors' because its narrow old streets lead into spacious squares where Paduans meet at pavement cafés to put the world right. Most cafés have their own locals according to political beliefs or cultural interests. The original 'café without doors' is still there – the Perocchi in piazza Cavour, where liberals met in the Renaissance and Garibaldi's liberal supporters met last century to plot for a free and united Italy.

Padua
continued

My favourite square is the beautiful Prato della Valle – oval 17th-century garden with statues of the famous and a circular waterway. It has been a Roman theatre, a field for tourneys and floral battles under Charlemagne, an airfield for balloons in 1808, then a trotting race track. Now it has an open-air market three times a week and in daytime, alas, parked cars. So look at it in the evening. To get the feel of Padua, go to the two market squares, piazza delle Erbe (vegetables), and piazza dei Frutti, separated by the huge Palazzo della Ragione (1218); it has a room 76 m (250 ft) long called the Salone, because it was a

meeting place of the communes once; delightful frescos. The Salone has a 'stone of dishonour' on which wrongdoers were exposed. The vegetable market with its remarkable variety is fascinating. Continentals are amazed at the edible plants we British ignore in our lush country. The ground floor of the Salone is packed with stalls selling cheeses, fresh meat and poultry, fish, from salted baccalà to live fish in an aquarium, and a mouthwatering variety of cured, smoked and raw sausages and meats. Get there 8-10 a.m. to see the housewives moving in.

A lot more to see, but don't miss 'Il Bo', the university founded in 1222 (the name comes from the old inn knocked down to build it, The Bull). Don't miss either the university hall with coats of arms of students and teachers, including John Tiptoft, Earl of Worcester – Latin lecturer here 1471-1509. Galileo held the chair in mathematics 1592-1610 and constructed his first telescope. Oliver Goldsmith was a student 1755-7. St Anthony's Cathedral and the Scrovegni chapel both have lovely frescos.

Along this road rich Venetians had their villas, in the valley of the Brenta river. At Strà is Villa Pisani ('Villa Strà'), one of the best in Italy; built in the 18th century for immensely rich Pisani family. Now it is called Villa Nazionale. In 1807 it was sold to Napoleon. Here Hitler met Mussolini in 1934. Wonderful decorations, including a ballroom ceiling by the older Tiepolo. Lovely park with a maze and fine scenes. Though you may be impatient to reach Venice, it is worth seeing this masterpiece.

Fly-drive Tuscany
**(Pisa, Tarquinia, Siena, Florence,
Montecatini Spa, Lucca, Viareggio, Pisa)**

Through varied scenery, this route takes you to see
some of Italy's greatest medieval and Renaissance
treasures. If you find too many to digest, it is easy to
cut a few corners and spend more time by the coast,
but it is well worth saving one overnight stop for
Siena and Lucca, and two for Florence.

From Pisa, follow the road S1 to Tarquinia (see Route
1). The route starts through drab industrial suburbs
but soon crosses hills, then runs into nice coastal
scenery, with woods and little side roads to bathing
beaches from Cecina onwards. Tarquinia, a
fascinating place, is little known to British
travellers.

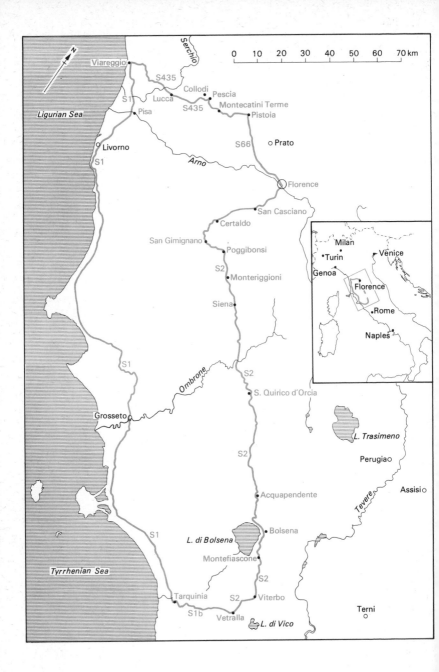

From Tarquinia, take local road to S1b to Vetralla, then S2 to Viterbo (45 km)

Viterbo – Zi Giulia, via Tuscanese: spit-roast game and meat. Meals L8,000–14,000.

Mini Palace Hotel, via Santa Maria della Grotticella (town outskirts): pleasant, low building with balconies; efficient bedrooms; no restaurant. Room L15,000–28,000. Good parking.

At La Quercia (3 km along S204 towards A1 motorway) – Aquilanti: country-style restaurant serving country dishes, like croutons of local ham, fettuccine (strip pasta of Rome area) and other home-made pastas including ravioli con ricotta, with cottage cheese and spinach; choice of grilled meats; zuppa inglese (*not* English soup but trifle). Excellent wine list. *Michelin* star. Meals L10,000–18,000. Closed Tuesdays.

The 'city of graceful fountains and lovely women' is surrounded by medieval walls; now really

two cities – the old, with glorious old streets, and the modern, built after war damage. Craftsmen still live among the alleys, courts and staircases of piazza San Pellegrino district. In piazza del Gesú, where a lively market is held, the younger Simon de Montfort and his brother Guy, returning from a crusade in 1271 (Friday the thirteenth), murdered the nephew of England's Henry III as he prayed at the altar and dragged him across the square by his hair in revenge for the killing of their father. The Montforts were excommunicated and their lands seized.

Popes dominated Viterbo's history, hiding here often

from Roman troubles. In piazza San Lorenzo a delicate tracery of open Gothic arches is all that is left of the papal palace loggia. Here Pope John XXI was arranging the downfall of monks he disliked when there was a clap of thunder and the roof fell in. Papal conclaves started here too. In the 13th century cardinals sat for over two years failing to choose a new pope, the governor locked them in this palace and took the roof off their room so that the Holy Spirit could come down to advise them. Then he stopped their rations. They chose quickly and wisely – Gregory X.

In Viterbo the historic meeting took place between Frederick Barbarossa, on his way to Rome to be crowned Holy Roman Emperor and the English Pope Hadrian IV (Nicholas Breakspear) in 1155. They met at the charming fountain in piazza della Morte and the Pope made the future Emperor hold his stirrup while he dismounted. Refusal would have meant no crown. It was a test of power.

La Cavalla da Cesare, via Bandita: the place to test the Est, Est, Est wine. Fine lake views from the terrace, country-style dining-room and cooking. Excellent pasta and roast meat (chicken, pork, veal); whitefish from the lake with salsa verde (sauce of parsley, onion, basil, capers, marjoram, anchovy and boiled eggs, with oil and lemon juice); small lake eels (beware, 13th-century Pope Martin IV died from eating too many Lake Bolsena eels, for which Dante placed him in purgatory in the *Divine Comedy*). Meals remarkable value at L8,000-10,000. Closed Wednesdays.

On a 180 m (600 ft) hillside above Lake Bolsena, surrounded by vines and stumps of volcanic hills; a near-legendary town of Italian wine. Bishop Fugger from an Augsburg banking family loved wine so much that he was called to Rome to answer for his overindulgence. He sent a servant ahead to mark inns which served good wine with the word *Est* – short for *Vinum est bonum,* the wine is good. At Montefiascone the man found a wine fuller than Frascati, subtler than Orvieto, with a better bouquet than the wines of Germany. So he wrote, *Est, Est, Est.* Bishop Johann Fugger agreed. He did not reach Rome. He drank himself to death at Montefiascone, asking that a barrel of the wine be poured over his grave. He is buried in San Flaviano church near the Roman gate of Montefiascone, with an epitaph beginning *Est, Est, Est.* And that is what the wine is still called. It is a little thin for a fat man like me. Unfortunately the church is being repaired and you may not be able to get in.

S2
Bolsena
(11 km)

Resort overlooking pleasant lake 68 km (42 miles) round. Old town is terraced up the hillside. Santa Christina, buried on lake island, went through some remarkable tortures unscathed after selling her Roman father's gods of silver and gold to feed the poor. She sang sweetly in a fire for five days, even after her tongue was cut out. Bathing beach and boat hire on lake, but crowded on weekends.

S2
Acquapendente
(34 km)

'Hanging Waters' – town on two sides of a chasm and divided by streams and waterfalls, fast flowing in spring, a trickle in midsummer. Rather a sombre town.

S2
Radiconfani
(31 km)

A land of woods, streams and few people. You climb and wind through the Paglia valley, with old bridges and hamlets, to this town on a rocky ridge which John Evelyn called 'a horrid rock'. There is a splendid panorama of southern Tuscany to Mount Amiata, a fact noted by a 13th-century refugee from Siena, Ghino di Tacco, who lived here with a gang of 400 who robbed or took 'tolls' from travellers between Rome and Siena. In *Decameron,* Boccaccio tells of how Ghino captured the Abbot of Cligny who was on his way to Rome to treat his indigestion at the baths. Ghino put him on a diet of dry toast, water and wine, which cured the overfed prelate so fast that he pleaded Ghino's cause with the Pope. Ghino was made a Knight of St John (the medical order) and given a palace to which he retired. But another robber-baron, Aldobrandeschi, had him murdered.

South-east, you can see from the town across the Umbrian Hills to the Apennines at 1,800 m (6,000 ft), beyond Assisi.

S2
Ripa d'Orcia
(23 km)

Downhill again to this village where, by turning left, you find at 3 km the ruined walls of Aldobrandeschi's castle, Castiglione d'Orchia, from which he took 'tolls' from Rome–Siena travellers. Must have been more costly to use via Cassia in medieval days than the motorways now.

S2
San Quirico
d'Orcia (5 km)

Pienza – Il Prato: good value; most people associate fritti misti with mixed fried fish, but it can be mixed meats, and here it includes local lamb and chicken. Good salami and ham. Meals L8,000-10,000. Closed Wednesdays and early July.

More medieval ramparts, town gate and houses. But a mere 9 km along S146 to the right is a splendid little planned town, Pienza. When it was called Corsignano in 15th century, a local lad, Aeneas Piccolomino, became Pope Pius II and commissioned Bernado, the Florentine

San Quirico
d'Orcia
continued

architect-sculptor, to build a city to rival Rome. Pius died six years later when only part was finished. Palazzo Piccolomini is ornately decorated and has fine views to the south. Cathedral in black and white marble contains Pius' throne. There are palaces, too, of the knights brought to his home village by this witty, learned man who was a patron of the arts but hardly humble, for he claimed direct descent from Romulus, founder of Rome, and was liberal with his coat of arms on local walls.

S2 Siena
(43 km)

See Route 2 – park and walk where possible.

S2
Monteriggioni
(15 km)

Il Pozzo: real country restaurant with local farm food nicely cooked, especially meat antipasto, panzerotti (a local ravioli), tagliatelle pasta, ham and pork. Meals L12,000. Closed Mondays and Sunday evening. Local Chianti Classico.

You may feel that you have seen enough medieval walled towns for now, but each is different. This village looks sinister on its steep hill, its 13th-century walls carrying fourteen towers. Still a working village to which farm workers return at night. Rich countryside round here, with vineyards, olives, orchards and good pastures.

S2
Poggibonsi

Lively little industrial town where they make the *fiasco* – raffia-covered bottles for Chianti wine.

local road to
San Gimignano
(11 km)

La Cisterna and Ristorante
La Terrazza, piazza della
Cisterna: magnificent
views, excellent food, very
popular, so telephone
(930328) or book; large
wooden-balconied rooms
in medieval style
overlooking valley;

Much-praised tourist
centre which has
disappointed some visitors
but not me, despite so many
guided groups walking
around. Impressive
approach, with thirteen
towers piercing the skyline;
two of Tuscany's most
attractive squares. In piazza
del Duomo are the
cathedral itself, with superb
frescos, including splendid
work by the great colour-
artist Ghirlandaio, and the
12th-century governor's
palace (Palazzo del
Podestà) and Palazzo del
Popolo with a 36 m (117 ft)
tower giving fine views
from the top, fine paintings
in its museum, and a
pleasant courtyard with old
brick paving and a well.

G.Gennai

San Gimignano
continued

restaurant on top floor serves real Tuscan dishes – also superb tortellini verdi (stuffed rings of pasta with hot cream sauce), tortelloni (like a large ravioli), risotto, excellent steak. Meals L10,000-15,000; rooms L15,000-30,000. Closed Tuesdays and January.

Bel Soggiorno: simple but all rooms have baths. Meals L7,000-10,000; rooms L18,000.

Wedding-night scenes in the frescos of the tower are sexy and earthy.

Also brick-paved is piazza della Cisterna, with 14th-century houses around an octagonal well. San Gimignano was a prosperous free city until local family and intercity wars drove it into anonymity under the banner of the Medicis in Florence. Once there were seventy towers, built by families to keep up with the Joneses. You had to own a merchant ship at Pisa to build one, but you were a nobody without a tower.

local road north to Certaldo (13 km)

Osteria del Vicario: flowered terrace; local food well cooked; noted for meat, especially lamb. Tourist menu L6,000; other meals L8,000-10,000. Five rooms from L12,000.

Old town of pink brick perched on a hill with views of the splendid Chianti countryside. Boccaccio, who wrote the *Decameron* in nearby Florence, died here. His house in the upper town, renewed after war damage, is a museum.

local road to San Casciano (through San Donato) (25 km)

Taste the Chianti at Il Fedino, via Fedino Borromeo: in an old villa; food is good value. Meals around L8,000.

The country of Chianti Classico, the best of the Chianti wines. Just before the town a little road left leads to Montepaldi, where the great Florentine family Corsini, once second in power to the Medicis, produce fresh white Tuscan wine and a very good Chianti intended for drinking young. Alas, the vineyards are too busy to receive casual visitors, though some small growers offer tastings along the roads of the Chianti country. Chianti wine is now all red. Some white used the title when I was a lad. The big Chianti Classico area runs down south almost to Siena, and Greve, 16 km (10 miles) south-east of Casciano, is one of the great centres, with Uzzano, producing excellent wine, near by. But the best is Brolio, nearer Siena, from the vineyards of Barone Ricasoli, whose forebear, an Italian prime minister, organized Chianti growers into a society to keep up standards.

**S2 Florence
(13 km)**

See Route 2.

**S66 to
Pistoia
(35 km),
Montecatini
Terme (15 km),
or use
motorway
from Florence
to Montecatini
Terme
(49 km)**

Montecatini, a resort, has dozens of hotels and restaurants of every grade. One of the best restaurants – Le Panteraie, via Panteraie: by no means the dearest; views from terrace. Meals L12,000-18,000. Swimming -pool; dancing. Closed Tuesdays and November-March.

Countryside here is a little depressed and the motorway gives almost as good views. Pistols are said to have been invented in Pistoia. Interesting narrow shopping street is via degli Orafi. German Gothic Line, last line of defence, ran through this area, so much was rebuilt after war damage.

Montecatini
continued

Montecatini, Italy's biggest and most fashionable spa, is attached to a commercial town. Spa itself is elegant, charming, expensive. Lofty halls of marble; fountains, pools for swimming and admiring, gardens, colonnades, almost every kind of sport from fashionable trotting races at midnight to pinball machines, a casino, of course (why do people trying to improve their health also try to ruin their fortunes?). The very pavements are made of marble in places – so are some loos. The five waters you can drink under medical supervision to alleviate twenty-four different ailments, from obesity and indigestion to liver complaints and infertility, are served from taps at a marble bar. They are called Tamerica, Torreta, Regina, Tettuccio and Rinfresco – rich in sulphates and bromine, and radioactive. Best not to gulp them in litres. The Romans discovered the spa. It is open from beginning of April until end of November.

At Monsummano
(S436 – 2 km) is a 'sweat'
cave, 400 metres long,
producing steam from a hot
lake; good for relieving
rheumatic ailments.
Hottest part, called the
inferno, was inevitably used
by Dante as a setting for his
Inferno.

S435 to Pescia, immediately after turn right for Collodi (15 km)	Beautiful terraced gardens of 18th-century villa. Baroque with fountains, water staircase, parterre flowerbeds; a small green theatre and bath-house where, invisible to each other, ladies and gentlemen could bathe, talk and listen to music. Open 8 a.m. to sunset. Villa, with fine furniture, is usually open, too. In the kitchen Carlo Lorenzini (called Collodi) first told stories of his puppet Pinocchio.
S435 Lucca (17 km)	One of Italy's finest old towns – see Route 1.
S435 Viareggio (29 km)	Lively, fashionable beach resort with many excellent restaurants – see Route 1.
S1 Pisa (21 km)	Fly-drive tours to Pisa, with cheap all-in car hire rates, are organized from Britain by CIT, 256 High Street, Croydon CR9 1LL; and British Airways (Freewheeler), West London Air Terminal, Cromwell Road, London SW7, in conjunction with Avis car hire.

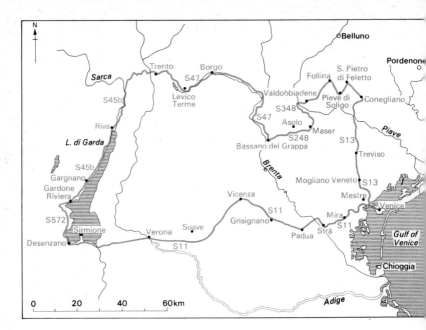

Fly-drive Venice

**(Venice, Padua, Vicenza, Verona,
Lake Garda, Trento, Bassano, Asolo, Treviso,
Venice)**

A superb holiday route with one pleasant surprise
after another. Though starting out rather badly in an
industrial belt, this route has remarkable variety in a
fairly small area. You see some of the greatest
artistic and historic cities in the world – Venice,
Padua, delightful little Vicenza and Verona, then you
can rest awhile from padding the old streets and
buildings at one of the small resorts on Lake Garda.
From Trento you can drive through magnificent
mountain scenery descending gradually to the
lusher hills of the Veneto, where the countryside is
just as superb, diverting to see Robert Browning's
delightful little hideaway at Asolo, then taking to the
little country roads of the wine routes, past farms
which lure you with promises of tastings. The driver
must be strong-willed until the evening.

Basically the route starts to follow Route 4, but in the
opposite direction, then takes to the shores of Lake
Garda on a beautiful road to join Route 3 but with
considerable diversions. So here I have filled in the
gaps and given the diversions.

Most travellers on a fly-drive tour like this would
almost certainly want to spend more time
sightseeing and browsing than those making for
Venice the travellers' way. You could drive this route
easily in a week and enjoy it, but you would inevitably
miss a lot, especially the atmosphere of the old cities
and villages. With a fortnight to spare, you could do
some justice to the cities, have time to take a
complete change from Renaissance art *and* put your
feet up beside Lake Garda.

Both British Airways and CIT offer money-saving fly-drive packages to Venice in conjunction with Avis hire-cars.

From Venice,
S11 through
Mira and
Strà to
Padua
(Padova)
(34 km)

See Route 4, but with more time, and if you are a Palladio enthusiast as I am, you could follow the Brenta canal down to Fusina on the lagoon to see Villa Malcontenta (Discontented), a mansion built in 1560 for the Foscari family. Legend says that the name came because one of the ladies of the family was banished here after being unfaithful to her husband. You can visit it and it has been superbly restored.

You can also take a boat trip down the Brenta canal from Strà passing many Palladian and other villas. You arrive back in Venice but they return you to your car at Strà by coach. A lovely trip even if in the wrong direction. Venetians who owned the villas used to be rowed along to the sound of music.

S11 Padua to
Vicenza (with
diversion to
Grisignano by
little road on
right) (34 km)

See Route 4.

S11 Vicenza to Verona (with small diversion to Soave on right) (57 km)	See Route 4.	
S11, very short diversion on right to Sirmione, then Desenzano (43 km)	See Route 4.	

S572, then
S45b Gardone
Riviera
(20 km)

Resort hotels and restaurants of all grades.

At Portese, 4 km south – Piero Bella: lakeside rustic restaurant with rooms; famous for its tortellini pasta and lake trout. Meals L10,000-14,000. Closed Mondays. Rooms L10,000-18,000. Open March-October.

At Gardone – Hotel Bellevue: in big villa; charming, fine service, excellent value; flower gardens and terrace overlooking lake. Meals L8,000-10,000. Closed Wednesdays. Rooms L10,000-18,000. Open April-October.

At Fasano, 2 km north-east – Hotel Fasano: pricy but good value, garden terrace overlooking lake; excellent seafood, especially lake fish. Meals L15,000. Closed Fridays. Rooms L29,000-45,000. Open May-September.

Most fashionable of the Garda lake resorts, though fairly quiet. Mild climate, lush vegetation, and Hruska botanical gardens, some of Europe's most interesting. Gabriele d'Annunzio, poet, Fascist, aesthete, novelist, lover-boy and heroic military commander who died in 1938, had a villa with gardens built here and it is worth seeing (Vittoriale estate). In summer, theatrical open-air performances are held in the park. Part of the town is spread along the lakeside, the rest spread over green hills. With his legionaries, d'Annunzio took and held the town of Fiume (Rijeka) against the Allies in 1919 and he and some of them are buried here in the prow of a ship.

S45b to
Gargnano
(12 km) then
Riva (29 km)

At Gargnano – La Tortuga: pricy, but one of the best restaurants in Lombardy. Speciality is bocconcini al tartufo nero – little pieces of veal stuffed with cheese and ham, with a sauce of 'Venus shell', locally called a sea truffle but I am told that we regard it as a form of cockle. Excellent lake fish with parsley. Meals L15,000-25,000 but more with 'Venus shell'. Closed Tuesdays and January-March.

The road along this shore is rich in bridges and tunnels and is pleasantly spectacular. Gargnano is a charming little place, centre of lemon and olive growing and among the best scenery on Lake Garda. Mussolini lived in Villa Feltrinelli between the time Italy joined the Allies in 1943 and until he fled in April 1945. See the attractive 13th-century church of San Francesco with adjoining cloisters. Just after three tunnels on road S45b, a branch road to Tignale (7 km) leads up to a church (Madonna di Monte Castello) perched nearly 700 m (2,000 ft) over the lake with a superb panoramic view.

Limone, outside town in quiet spot on S45b – Panorama: big restaurant with fine views. Menu (3-course) L6,000. Good value.

Limone, where figs and honey are produced, is a little fishing port between rocky hills. Has many hotels and restaurants, so full in summer.

At Riva – Hotel Luise, viale Roverto: modern, pleasant, large garden, pool, 150 metres from lake shore; some rooms have shower but no WC, others have both. Good meals L8,000-13,000. Closed Fridays. Rooms L15,000-25,000. Open April–September.

Riva is a lovely town – medieval buildings including a 12th-century castle, surrounded by moats; it is a neat and tidy town, with Monte Rochetta to the west and superb gardens to the east – with an avenue of magnolias.

Villa Nicolli: small, modern, family run, friendly; good cooking, but dearer than Hotel Luise.

Lido Palace, viale Carducci:
excellent value for old,
traditional 'grand hotel'.
Well-tended gardens, pool,
charming public rooms.
Meals L8,000-10,000;
closed Mondays; rooms
L25,000-35,000. Open
April–October.

S45b Trento (50 km)	See Route 3.	Magnificent lake and mountain scenery, and road not difficult.
S47 Levico, Terme, Borgo, Bassano del Grappa (88 km)	See Route 3.	Route a little less attractive around Bassano but superb at Asolo.

S248, then small turning to the left to Asolo (18 km)

Villa Cipriani: very pricy but very charming and splendid cooking; until recently run by the Cipriani family of Venice, one of the greatest restaurant families in the world. Fine dishes include a typical Cipriano risotto. Excellent wine list as well as Guinness, not unconnected with the fact that the Guinness family once owned it. Pretty house, magnificent views from terrace and most bedrooms. Don't settle for a room on the road if you can avoid it. Meals L16,000-24,000. Closed Mondays November–April. Rooms L46,000-84,000. Lovely garden.

One of my favourite little towns in Europe, and Robert Browning felt the same. He lived there and it was a silk-spinning maid from Asolo who sang: 'God's in his heaven, all's right with the world' in his poem 'Pippa Passes' as she crossed the market square. The square is still there, complete with fountain and lions of the Venetian Republic. And Asolo still has magic within its medieval walls, where narrow winding streets are porticoed against rain and sun through which you can see its surrounding hills dotted with white farm houses. Villa Cipriani, now a hotel, was once Browning's

Asolo
continued

Locanda due Mori da Dante, piazzetta E. Duse: country dishes nicely cooked; tagliatelle a ragú (like Bolognese), mushroom risotto, pasta with beans and tripe 'soup' (stewed, and better than it sounds). Also excellent local cured pork sausage, bacon, chicken; meals around L10,000. Closed Wednesdays and one August week.

Duse: pleasant medium-priced hotel. Meals pricy L15,000-22,000. Closed Mondays. Rooms L24,000-36,000.

Osteria Ca Dentin, via Mazzolini: neat, clean, serving good meals at fair prices. I had excellent guinea fowl (faraona). Meals L8,000-10,000.

house, and he left it to his son.

'The town of a hundred horizons', an Italian poet called it. Two towers beside a garden are all that is left of the castle of Caterina Cornaro, who held court here for twenty years from 1489. She was 'persuaded' by the Doge to cede the strategic isle of Cyprus, of which she was Queen, to the Venetian Republic in return for a 'kingdom' in Italy. They gave her Asolo! You can see Browning's other house almost opposite the lovely little 16th-century Zen fountain on the street called via Roberto Browning. Many more beautiful old villas line the streets. You can visit, too, Eleonora Duse's house, a room in the civic museum containing mementos of this actress and her tomb in the churchyard of Santa Anna. A Venetian who made her name around the world as one of the greatest actresses ever, she died in 1924. Asolo still produces handworked furniture, embroidery, wrought iron and silks, and the embroidery school was founded by Browning's son.

S248, then road to left to Maser (6 km)

Villa di Maser, originally called Villa Barbero as it was built for the Barbero brothers, is one of Palladio's greatest inspirations. Long,

low and both decorative and elegant, it is decorated inside with some absolutely magnificent frescos by Paolo Veronese (1528-88), including the cycle of Venus and Apollo, Bacchus, and the gods on Mount Olympus, covering a ceiling. Also some fine stuccoes by Alessandro Vittoria, who also decorated Palladio's Tempietto (Little Temple) in the park. Veronese frescoed the Grotto of Neptune in the garden. The villa is lived in, but is open 3-6 p.m. on Tuesdays, Saturdays and Sundays, June to September, and 2-5 p.m. same days in other seasons. Really worth waiting in Asolo an extra day so as not to miss it. In the grounds is museum of old cars and carriages.

from Maser, back on to S248 for a very short distance, then left on to S348; about 12 km along it a right turn over river Piave takes you to Valdobbiadene (about 24 km from Maser)

Valdobbiadene: Diana, via Roma: very adequate hotel with good-value restaurant to try local wines and game. Has won an Italian cooking award. Meals L10,000; closed Fridays; rooms L15,000-23,000. Closed January.

Valdobbiadene is the centre of Prosecco and other sparkling white wines of Veneto. From there you are following the White Wine Road (Strada del Vino Bianco) over and round vine-clad hills, through little villages, with farms offering tastings, with cured bacon

Valdobbiadene
continued

Albergo Alla Torre, via Mazzolini: excellent grill restaurant with steaks, chops, fish cooked over charcoal. Very good tagliatelle. Meals L6,000-8,000 – excellent value.

and sausage which dangle from hooks in the ceiling, and rough home-made bread. Delicious! You will find the best ones by venturing on to the little side roads. Tablewine, young and refreshing if not in the best Soave class. Follina has a 13th-century abbey; Pieve wines are good and its pork and game dishes excellent; San Pietro has a 14th-century church with interesting Romanesque and 16th-century frescos.

then local roads: take road towards Vittorio Follina, then right-hand road to Pieve di Soligo, road north-east winding round to San Pietro di Feletto on to Conegliano (about 54 km)

Pieve di Soligo – Alla Colombo, via Capodivillia: have not been there recently, but used to serve good meals and had a long wine list of local, other Italian and French wines. Old building, bright and breezy welcome. Meals L10,000-14,000; simple but adequate rooms L8,000-15,000.

Conegliano, centre for supplying Venice with much of its white and red wine, game and pork products; also asparagus and a local type of lettuce.

Tre Panoce, via Vecchia: old country-house style restaurant whose *padrone* uses his experience of working in well-known restaurants in Rome and Milan to produce some

Conegliano: little known to Britons but well known to Venetians. Most pleasant place surrounded by hills, orchards and vineyards, called by one writer *ridente* – smiling. Lovely view from grounds of castle (mostly destroyed in First World War – this is the area of very fierce fighting between Italians and Austrians). Via 20 Settembre is a superb street lined with

delightful meals. Good use of fresh vegetables and salad from the area. Garden. Meals L12,000–16,000. Closed Mondays and August.

Canon d'Oro, via 20 Settembre: pleasant, historic old restaurant, most famous of many in this street. Mostly Venetian-style cooking, with excellent risotto using ingredients in season; also good pasta, excellent vegetables and a good choice of local wines. Meals L8,500–12,000; closed Saturdays; rooms L13,000–21,000.

Renaissance 'palaces' and nice pavement cafés. In the cathedral, dedicated to the Madonna of the Flagellants in 1352, is a fine painting by the local artist G. B. Cisma (1460–1518) who brought the local hill scenery into colourful paintings which have been compared to Giovanni Bellini. Sala dei Battuti (Chamber of the Flagellants) can be visited by applying to the sacristan; it is decorated with frescos.

Strada del Vino Rosso (Road of Red Wine) runs southwards crossing Piave river at Ponte di Piave, on to Roncade, but is a longer way to Treviso than ours, if more refreshing.

S13 Treviso (28 km)

S13 to Venice via Mogliano-Veneto and Mestre (30 km)

See Route 3 – please don't forget that Treviso is an interesting place and that Villa Condulmer at Mogliano-Veneto is an outstanding, if pricy, hotel, so try to leave a little more time for this final run-in.

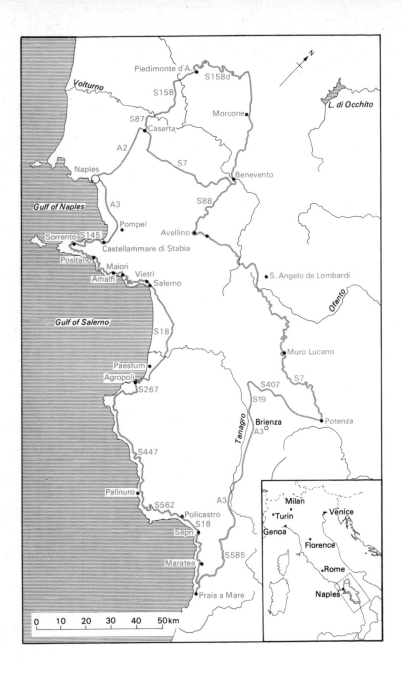

Fly-drive Naples

(Naples, Vesuvius, Pompeii, Sorrento, Amalfi drive, Paestum, Potenza, Benevento, Caserta, Naples)

Most tourists hug the coast south from Naples, going as far as Salerno southwards, and cut inland only as far as Caserta to the north. But there is some spectacular and interesting country in the mountains, and not all the roads are hard work. Most of the mountainous middle of this route, through the centre of Italy, is little known even to Italians. But there are motorway short cuts if you tire a little.

Hotels and restaurants tend to be better near the coast as this has been tourist country for three generations. The people who would now fly to the Caribbean used to winter in Sorrento and Positano, and many big hotels used to shut altogether in summer.

Naples claims to have invented the pizza and believes that they must be baked in an open wood-fired oven in front of you, made with bread dough and filled only with tomato, mozzarella cheese, anchovies, chopped basil, wild marjoram (origano) and olive oil. Pizza rustica is quite different – a flan filled with a mixture of cheese, eggs, and ham or sausage in a cream sauce. The local spaghetti has a rather watery tomato sauce (called al pomodoro) but a better dish is spaghetti al filetto di pomodoro – sauce made with whole fresh tomatoes.

In Naples itself, the word vermicelli is used for spaghetti and not for the much thinner pasta eaten elsewhere.

The wine of Vesuvius' slopes, Lacrima Christi (Tears of Christ) comes in red, white (medium dry) and rosé (rosato). Locals say that a German expert, tasting it, fell on his knees and cried: 'Oh, Christ, why did you not cry in Germany?' But our own Victorian expert Professor Saintsbury said it tasted like lemonade stirred with a chocolate bar. Naples produced recently the notorious wine which, analysed by the University of Bologna, was shown to be made mostly from the scrapings of banana boats and contained no grape juice. But there are absolutely genuine local wines, palatable and cheap, if not great. Good wines include red Taurasi, rough when young, velvety and full when three or four years old – from Avellino – and Ravello rosso, a dry red with sweet aftertaste. The Salerno Medical School, founded AD 1000, announced: 'To keep healthy begin your supper with wine, and with every egg drink a glass of wine.'

From Naples (see Fly-drive Calabria) take motorway A3 to Castellamare di Stabia (29 km)

A chance to see Vesuvius, the mountain whose eruption covered the town of Pompeii with volcanic ash – people, dogs, and all – in AD 79, and the remains of Pompeii itself, surely the most remarkable, moving and interesting ancient site in Europe. Don't go up Vesuvius on a hot summer's day unless you have very strong lungs.

S145, S163 along coast to Sorrento (19 km)

Marina di Equa – Le Axidie: Fernando Savarese's hotel is one of my favourites in Europe. Not deluxe, but very comfortable, friendly, quiet, excellent cuisine, young wine from own vineyard; private beach, tennis court; pool; pleasant atmosphere.

Vico Equense on this road is no longer the charming little-known place of fifteen years ago. The motorcar has won. But the busy main square is fun for sitting outside a café watching the scene. And if you stick to the coast road, avoiding

Open April-October. Meals L13,000; rooms L30,000-43,000.

Hotels, *pensioni,* restaurants, *trattorie* of all kinds in Sorrento.

Pleasant family-run *pensione* is Dania, via Calata Puolo: 3 km from centre, in orange and lemon groves, with small paths down to a rocky beach. Open April-October. Meals L7,000-8,000; rooms L10,000-15,000.

La Favorita O'Parrucchiano, corso Italia: best value restaurant here; excellent fish and fish soup, of course; in casa (home-made) dishes only; fine local cheeses (trecce, scamorzine, mozzarella), and fresh vegetables. Meals L8,000-11,000. Closed Wednesdays in low season.

modern flyovers, you will find, as you leave, a tiny road on the right to the sea, leading to the fishing village of Marina di Equa, with a superb little hotel, a few bars and a genuine fishing fleet. It's a smuggling village too. I have seen it happen.

Sorrento has been the true tourist resort of the area for 150 years. Crowded tourist cafés and restaurants, souvenir shops, but good general shopping, bathing below cliffs and a likable place which grows on you.

At Sorrento Point (2 km) is superb view of Bay of Naples and Gulf of Sorrento.

S145 to Positano, Amalfi, Atrani, Minori, Maiori, Vietri, Salerno (68 km)

Positano: plenty of *pensioni* and restaurants to choose from – Buca di Bacco: best known restaurant; excellent but pricy. Meals L11,000-18,000. Open March-October.

My discovery is Trattoria Giardino Degli Aranci (just past main car park, in lane to right, as the main road begins to climb to leave town): family run; truly excellent home-made pasta and fresh fish. Meals L6,000-8,000.

The famous Amalfi drive. Beautiful; hard work for the driver round sharp, narrow bends – hoot loudly! Superb.

Positano: down steep side road; most attractive but terribly crowded in season. Parking not easy.

Salerno
continued

Da Vincenzo, by Casa Sopriano: a shop with bar and tables where you eat well and cheaply. Around L6,000.

Amalfi – La Caravella: excellent cooking and outstanding value; spaghetti Caravella, with a sauce of prawns, little octopus, anchovies, garlic, and tomato; great grilled fish; fish soup; fried anchovies in a fine sauce; good white wine – Ravello di San Marco. Meals L7,000-10,000. Closed Tuesdays off-season.

Miramalfi: new, good-class hotel against a cliff, high above sea with fine views. Pool and lift to shore. Rooms with restricted view are cheapish. Good cuisine. Meals L10,000; closed Tuesdays; rooms L17,000-35,000.

Amalfi: though tourist packed, it is beautiful; a one-off place. Oldest of Italian maritime republics (6th century), later its fleet of galleys carried the Crusaders to Levant. A Saracen tower; 12th- to 16th-century Capuchin monastery (now Hotel Luna Torre Saracena); 11th-century cathedral with Romanesque tower dominating a lovely square. Longish pebbly beach is highly organized. Famous for its fish restaurants.

Ravello: reached through hairpin bends from Amalfi up superbly panoramic road above the sea, with stairways, steep alleys and roofed passages up the slopes of Dragon Hill.

Atrani: fishing village at end of Dragon Valley; not so many tourists; 10th-century church.

Minori – Saint Lucia: nice cheap hotel. Meals L6,000-8,000; rooms L10,000-15,000. Open March-November.

Minori: charming village with beach and watchtowers at each end. Relaxed.

Maiori: deservedly but unfortunately become very popular. Beach, night life. Background of lemon and orange gardens.

Vietri: white houses, shady streets, little shops, beach. Famous for pottery with strong Moorish influence.

Salerno – see Fly-drive Calabria route.

S18
Paestum
(48 km)

Old Greek colony with beautiful Doric temples hardly surpassed in Greece itself. You do not need to be a Greek scholar to appreciate this site. Large and well-preserved, the temples are more impressive than their descriptions or photographs. Museum packed with interesting treasures. City was originally called Poseidonia. It became Roman, then Christian, but the people were driven out by malaria and Saracen raiders. When underground temples to Hera were uncovered in 1954, honey was found in bronze vases almost perfect.

S18 for 4 km, then right on to S267 to Agropoli (7 km)	Carola e Splendid: good restaurant, especially for fish. Meals L7,500-10,000; closed Tuesdays; rooms L10,000-17,000.	Don't continue on the S18 to Palinuro. Though marked as a main road it no longer has a right to be. The surface is appalling – rutted, pot-holed, bent, and as it climbs and zigzags it can be dangerous. Not very interesting, either. Few Italians use this road. It is worth a few minor hold-ups on the coast road to avoid it. Agropoli is a pretty place with a little old harbour and has a bar and two simple restaurants.
S267, then S447 to Palinuro	On S447 – Saline Hotel: modern; no single rooms. Meals L12,000; rooms L32,000-44,000. Pool; air-conditioning; next to sandy beach.	A strip of coast hardly known to Britons. Choice of beaches, excellent for underwater swimming. Uncommercialized and friendly.
S562 to Policastro S18 to Sapri, Maratea, Praia Mare (76 km)	See Fly-drive Calabria route.	Scenic drive to Policastro.
S585 to join A3 motorway (34 km)	See Fly-drive Calabria route.	
A3 northwards to Brienza, then on to S19 northwards until it joins S407 to Potenza (94 km)	Potenza – Fuori le Mura, via 4 Novembre: country dishes, such as sopressate, the super garlic sausage, mountain cheeses and soft dairy sauces, a nice 'peasant' sauce to the ravioli, and a good local tripe dish – if you like tripe. Meals L8,000-10,000.	Superb scenery on this motorway route. Potenza is rather a dull town in itself but is the gateway to Lucania, the wild and rugged mountain country which very few tourists visit.

Tourist Hotel, via
Vescovado: clean, family-
run, family cooking. Meals
L8,000; rooms L12,000-
16,000.

S7 to
Muro Lucano
(49 km)
Sant'Angelo
dei Lombardi
on to Avellino
(total 160 km)

Muro Lucano – Delle
Colline: excellent cooking of
fresh country food, quite a
find. Meals from L7,000;
simple rooms L8,000-
10,000.

The old Appian Way, which
some of our forefathers
drove along in much more
primitive cars than ours. A
zigzag route through
remarkable mountain
scenery. A bit tiring, so take
it easily with rests and
walkabouts. More eccentric
bits are just after Muro
Lucano, which has an
artificial lake. An interesting
little town, where Hannibal
and Marcellus fought a
battle in 210 BC. In the
castle, now in ruins, Joanna
I, Queen of Naples who
collected husbands, was
suffocated in her bed in
1382. Her body was taken
to Naples on an ass to be
exhibited. Sant'Angelo, on
a hill with good views, was
founded by the Lombards
and has many Renaissance
buildings.

Avellino

Known for its hand-made
pasta, cheeses, cakes and
pastries, so watch your
weight.

Jolly Hotel, via Tuoro
Cappuccini: one of the
group started by a textile
industrialist for travelling
businessmen and reps;
efficient, little character,
good value. Meals L9,500;
rooms L25,000-35,000.

Avellino: in a green valley of
woodland and hills,
bounded by mountains;
12th-century cathedral with
later neo-classical façade.
Pottery school.

Avellino
continued

Da Tonino Martella, via Trinità: unassuming restaurant with local dishes. Meals L5,000–8,000. Closed Thursdays.

S88
Benevento
(36 km)

Pascalucci, piano Capelle: old farm made into a happy restaurant where you feel one of the family, so service is friendly if not de luxe. Home cooking, including good pasta made on the spot, grills, roast rabbit and lamb. Meals from L6,000.

Vecchia America, piano Cappelle: started by an Italian who emigrated to the USA, came back in the war, and bought the restaurant. Now run by his nephew. Good fusilli, local pasta, and roast pork, lamb or rabbit. Meals L7,000–10,000.

A fine town, in pleasant countryside, with a lot to see – and taste: centre of Strega liqueur, green or yellow, and nougat. See Roman theatre, one of the oldest existing, built in 2nd century under Emperor Hadrian; the splendid Trajan arch, built AD 114 in thanks to the Emperor for building the road via Traina; the cathedral, originally 7th century, destroyed in 1944, rebuilt with original façade. Santa Sofia church and cloisters, part of a Benedictine abbey founded in 8th century, with Moorish-style arcades, 8th-century paintings. A rewarding town.

if short of time take S7 to Caserta (33 km), a beautiful but longer route is: S17 to beyond Morcone, S158d to Piedimonte d'Alife then S158 and S87 to Caserta (133 km)

Longer route is scenic and, particularly after leaving S17, unspoiled, and you meet few travellers. S158b stretch is beautiful but windy and hilly and rather hard driving.

Caserta Vecchia – La Castellana: nicest restaurant around here. Signora Farina and family prepare some splendid dishes with

On this stretch you pass Monte Miletto on your right. Quite a diversion, but here you see something of truly 'unknown' Italy.

excellent sauces; try the pasta, antipasto in abundant helpings, but above all the minestra marinata – meat soup containing pork and vegetables and a small meal in itself. Meals around L10,000.

Da Teresa, via Torre: simple; excellent pastas and pizza. Meals L7,000.

Caserta town – Antica Locanda Massa-1848, via Mazzini: founded 1848 and still serving typical southern Italian dishes, with lots of melanzane (aubergine) and mozzarella cheese, including a pasta sauce containing both. Excellent meat dishes such as steak

Caserta is superb. Royal palace was built for the Bourbon kings of Naples and Sicily by Vanitelli from 1752 to 1774 because Charles III wanted a house to rival Versailles. It does not *quite* succeed, but it is a noble building and the inside is impressive. A vestibule decorated with statues leads to courtyards and a magnificent 'staircase of honour'. With its statues and pillars, and 116 marble steps, it looks as if it was built for a Hollywood historical musical. It is rumoured that when the palace was the headquarters of Anglo-American command in Italy in the Second World War,

Caserta
continued

cooked with cheese and ham, like a costolette alla Bolognese, but with beef instead of veal. Most interesting.

King George VI fell down this staircase on an official visit. Horrified British staff officers believed that they had lost their King, but he was undamaged. Field-Marshal Alexander received the German surrender in Italy here in 1945.

I love the French-designed park of fountains, ponds, islands, trees and hedges, with one huge cascade from a height of 78 m (256 ft) falling from a grotto. The English garden is of winding paths, cypress trees, cedars, flowers and even artificial ruins.

Few people bother to go to the old town, Caserta Vecchia, 10 km away, but it is a nice quiet medieval town with a 12th-century cathedral with more than a touch of Moorish influence.

from Caserta, motorway A2 to Naples

Fly-drive Calabria

(Naples, Salerno, Paola [for Lamezia Airport], Cosenza, Crotone, Catanzaro, Reggio, Tropea, Amalfi drive, Naples)

Almost an explorers' route. 'Excuse my ignorance,' said a journalist colleague, 'but where *is* Calabria?' Roughly, it is the toe and instep of Italy, but this trip takes us from Naples through much of Campania first.

Until the big motorway from the north, Autostrada del Sole, was finished quite recently, people went unwillingly to Calabria. Now other roads have been improved, hotels built by the sea and some British tour operators, especially Sovereign and the Italian-owned CIT, arrange inclusive holidays to a few resorts. But the rest of the country, especially inland, is little changed, and it is still wise to know which roads to avoid, because pot-holes, bends and steep slopes make them hard work, not fun.

Some of this route requires fairly hard driving and in the mountains you may not average much more than twenty m.p.h. Much of the scenery is rugged and harshly beautiful, and the heat in midsummer can be intense at beach resorts. But the mountains are cooler.

Some inland villages and towns are frankly primitive; nearly all towns are poorer than further north. Although hotels and restaurants are clean and serviceable, few have the same facilities as, for instance, those near Venice or in Tuscany. But for anyone who genuinely wants to get away from crowds and to see something entirely new in Europe, this is a really rewarding tour. The mountains are impressive and almost mystic, the coast varies from big beaches to rocky coves. British Airways and CIT both offer fly-drive arrangements to Naples, tied up with Avis cars, and CIT have some similar fly-drive

arrangements using the new airport of Lamezia, at St Eufemia Lamezia, which saves time but cuts off some nice drives at the beginning and end of the Naples route.

Of local food, fish is good, especially red mullet, swordfish and mountain trout. Try also sopressata, a sausage of cured pork; melanzane farcite, aubergine stuffed with anchovy and tomato, flavoured with garlic; and pasta alla Calabrese, local pasta with ginger-flavoured tomato sauce. Pastas come in elaborate shapes and with strange names, like sicchie li prieviti (priests' ears) and ricci di donna (lady's curls).

Good cheeses include soft mozzarella, as used by Neopolitans for the pizza; provola, which should be made with buffalo milk; and a spicy, firm but soft caciocavallo. Wines are drinkable but not exciting. Some, like the red Ciro di Calabria, come dry and sweet, so watch the label. Pellaro is dry, light red and potent.

from Naples take A3 motorway to Vesuvius, Pompeii and Salerno (56 km)

Naples is a crazy city to an outsider and fun if you keep a tight hold on your handbag or camera, another hand on your wallet or preferably don't carry any of these things. Also those stories of bag snatching by youths on motorbikes and general thievery are true, and even a locked car is not immune. If there is nothing else in it, they will snatch the radio. A pity, because Naples is the sort of place to walk the streets and view the scene and the people. Its treasures are so many that you must read a city guidebook and choose which you want to visit; but places I would not miss are the Capodimonte palace, not only for its superb paintings but its park, its furniture in the first floor royal apartments and its Brussels tapestries. I would see Santa Lucia suburb, with its seashore promenade and wonderful fish restaurants, and, although it is another tourist cliché, would certainly not miss the old Palazzo Reale (royal palace) for its incredibly beautiful furnishings and art treasures. Many Italian cities have traffic and parking problems. Naples traffic can be sheer hell, and

I know strong men and experienced drivers who pick up their hire cars at the airport and get straight out of it on the motorway so as to keep their tempers intact. The motorway passes right by Pompeii and that is something I would not miss even if I missed Vesuvius, the bad-tempered mountain which did the damage to this Roman town so long ago.

Salerno	Antica Pizzeria del vicolo della Neve, vicolo della Neve: in old town, genuine local restaurant with good fish and pizza. Good value. Meals L8,000.	Salerno is a chaotic city, with little to lure you to stay.
A3 motorway to just before Lagonegro (121 km) then turn right on to S585 to Praia a Mare (34 km)	Praia a Mare, I Normanni (1½ km south at Fiuzzi): very good restaurant; a few practical rooms. Meals L8,000-12,000; rooms L14,000-25,000.	Once you are clear of Salerno suburbs this motorway goes through superb mountain scenery and is very much easier to drive than the ordinary main roads, which negotiate some passes the hard way. A pleasant run down to the sea on S585 with several little trattorias of varying grades used also by lorry drivers. Praia is a pleasant little beach town; boats cross to the isle of Dino; coves and caves. You are now in Calabria.
S18 Scalea (12 km)	Talao Hotel: by far south standards, an absolute little winner. Nice clean rooms; pleasant owners and staff; good, if not brilliant, food. Meals L9,000; rooms L12,000-20,000. Swimming pool.	Scalea is set just back from a big beach and dominated by an old castle; it has a lively old centre. Also a few big hotels like Santa Caterina hotel-sporting complex with British and German package tourists.
S18 to Belvedere and Paola (60 km)	Alhambra Hotel, above town on S18: a good hotel with modern rooms, efficiently run and pleasant meals, including very good pasta. You can eat for L6,000; rooms L15,000-30,000.	Road runs along and above the coast, with a series of little seaside resorts in coves off to the right. Paola is a small historic town, truly Calabrian, set above a beach. At first glance it looks a bit seedy but you soon realize it is an old place needing a fresh coat of paint. A pretty little

Byzantine cathedral, and near by is the Sanctuary of St Francis of Paola, who founded the charitable Franciscan Order of Minims. Behind it are the mountains, with Crocetta Pass only 3,700 m (12,000 ft) from the sea and 113 m (3,700 ft) high and nearby Monte Cucuzzo almost as near the sea and 154 m (5,055 ft) high.

If flying to Lamezia Airport and picking up your car there, drive north along the coast up S18 to Amantea, Fiumefreddo to join the Naples route at Paola.

from Paola, turn inland on S107, then, before reaching motorway A3, turn right again into Cosenza

Imperiale Hotel, viale Trieste: large, with garage; restaurant gives good value. Specializes in soups, local pasta with odd names like 'fusilli', and local cheeses. Meals around L8,000; rooms medium priced. Restaurant closed Sundays.

La Calavrisella, via Gerolamo da Rada: best known restaurant; with its own special dishes, including very good stuffed veal. Wine from its own vineyards. Good value. Closed Saturday and Sunday evenings. Meals from L6,000.

Lovely views of mountains and sea. You might find treasure in Cosenza – under the bed of the Busento river. That is where his warriors buried King Alaric of the Visigoths, who sacked Rome in AD 410 and died here on his way to Sicily and North Africa. His loot was buried with him.

A pleasant and interesting town with old town climbing up the hill topped by a Norman castle where Charles V of France's brother, Louis of Anjou, married Margaret of Savoy. Inside the cathedral, started in 1185, is a lovely French Gothic tomb to Isabella of Aragon, wife of King Philip the Bold of France, who was son of St Louis. She was returning with her

Cosenza
continued

husband from an abortive
crusade in Tunisia where
her father-in-law had been
killed when she fell off a
horse and died giving birth.
Not a very happy trip for the
French royal family. At the
top of the town is a fine
terraced garden of Villa
Communale facing the Sila
foothills.

S19 along
Busento river
for 8 km, then
left on to S178
to Aprigliano,
alongside
Lake Arvo
S108b and on
to S107 to
San Giovanni
in Fiore
(61 km)

San Giovanni – Dino's: I
have had a good meal here,
with mountain pork
sausage, ham and fish from
nearby waters. Meals
L8,500. Modern rooms
L12,000-22,000. Disco.
Closed May.

A lovely climb into the Sila
mountains through
chestnut and oak woods on
a reasonable road. Almost
Swiss scenery, true
mountain villages, a lake of
placid water and in San
Giovanni the essence of
Calabria which you find up
here rather than at the
coast. It is the heart of the
Sila mountains.

S107 to
San Severina
and Crotone
(71 km)

Descent through rocky
valleys, then through
chestnut woods to olive
groves. San Severina is a
quiet little town high on a
cliff, with fine Byzantine
buildings. Nearing Crotone
are lovely views of the
Ionian coast.

Crotone

Costa Tiziani, 3 km south-
east: well-designed holiday
hotel complex with pool,
sports and some
entertainment where you
can stay overnight. Used by

Hard to think of modern
Crotone, an industrial town
with a pleasant seaside
resort, as one of the great
towns of ancient Greece,
famous for its philosophers,

CIT for air package holidays from Britain. Beach. Meals L10,000; rooms L20,000-35,000.

Bella Romagna, via Poggioreale: a *Michelin*-starred restaurant in Calabria! Alas, I have not tried it. Meals L12,000-20,000. Closed Mondays.

Il Girarosto, via Vittorio Veneto: good value, local dishes including excellent fish. Try mustica (little local fish marinated in oil and

artists, poets, medical men and especially its Olympic athletes – the site of the city decreed by the Doric oracle. But this part of Calabria was, in the 6th century BC, the Greek colony of Magna Graecia. Somewhere near by was Sybaris, the town of fine living where cooks were especially honoured and which gave us the word 'sybarite' for high-living. Sadly, Crotone defeated and exterminated it, and archaeologists still seek the remains. Crotone's most famous athlete, Milo, is said to have run round the stadium with a bull on his shoulders, killed it with his fist and then eaten it! It still has a superb Doric column standing alone beside the sea (12 km) – all that is left of the great temple of Hera, goddess and queen of the heavens. A 16th-century cathedral in the square of Pythagoras, who lived here, and a 16th-century castle built by the ruling Spanish to keep out the Turks.

Crotone
continued

peppers – deliciously savoury); also swordfish (pescespada) cooked in oil with herbs (very tasty). Surprisingly good wines, including Pellaro, light but strong red. Excellent value. Meals L8,000-12,000.

S106
coast road to
Marina di
Catanzaro
(70 km)

Road past rocky beaches and headlands, hilltop villages, and *fiumare* – riverbeds, usually dry but which in spring bring torrents down from the mountains and are the curse of Calabria, taking away vital water, livestock, top soil, and even houses in a few hours. Capo Rizzulto (7 km to left) and Il Castello (2 km), castle beside holiday hotel-village, worth a diversion.

Catanzaro – Hotel Guglielmo, via Tedeschi: air-conditioned, comfortable, central. Meals L9,000-14,000; closed Sundays; rooms L25,000-35,000.

At Marina di Catanzaro – Restaurant la Brace attached to Still Hotel: very good value; excellent fish, including mixed fried fish and fried sardines; also mustica (tiny fish in rich marinade). Especially known for its home-made macaroni. Nice Borgia white wine. Meals from L8,000; fine meal for L12,000; rooms L14,000-28,000.

Cropani Marina is a possible halt for a bathe or rest. Turn inland at Catanzaro marina to Catanzaro itself (14 km), the regional capital, the old Byzantine part looking rather decrepit but interesting. Villa Trieste has public gardens with a beautiful view to the sea and a museum of coins and paintings. Many old churches, including San Domenico with a fine painting in the rosary chapel. Lido has a good beach; 2 km away, in olive groves, the ruins of Roccelletta, 11th-century Norman church, still impressive.

S106 for 8 km, local coast road through Lido di Copanello, back on to S106 just before Soverato (33 km)

Copanello: Motel Copanello: simple, comfortable, nice position. Meals L10,000; rooms L10,000-22,000.

Soverato: fair choice of hotels and restaurants – Gli Ulivi, via San Giovanni Bosco: quiet, air-conditioned; open May-September. Meals L8,000-12,000; rooms L15,000-27,000.

On road into resort – A Lumera: good value; fine fish. Meals L7,000-11,000. Closed Tuesdays.

Copanello is a pleasant little resort with fine sand, backed by unspoilt, rather wild country; big holiday village. Rocks, inlets and little caves near by make it fine for underwater swimming. Just inland up a hill at Staletti is a wonderful spot for a longer, very quiet self-catering holiday, Villa Caluzzi. Ralph Caluzzi's father emigrated to the USA from this hamlet, became a chemist with a chain of stores. Young Ralph arrived back in 1943 as a US army sergeant, bought a farm, made superb little bungalows out of the old farm buildings with his own hands and still lives there happily, renting them to visitors for a week or more.

Soverato is a growing but still small resort with fine sandy beach and good views from old town.

S106 to Locri (65 km)

Pferdestall, contrada Capozza: one of the better cheaper restaurants, known for good meat. Meals around L8,000.

Coast road past a series of small resorts by old villages, like Rocella, perched on a rock by a castle; and Siderno, with 16th-century walls. Locri looks disappointing at first. But see the extensive remains of the Greek colony just out of town, and Gerace, a town on a rock with splendid views – 11 km inland. It is rich in treasures; see especially the 11th-century cathedral with ancient columns stolen from a Greek temple and 15th-century sculptures inside. An army of 52,000 Saracens once besieged Gerace in vain but the Norman Guiscard brothers from Hauteville took it, fought each other over it; they conquered a lot of the world. I would not miss Gerace.

S106 round coast to Reggio di Calabria (98 km)

Conti, via Giulia: I found it good; locals think it the best restaurant here. Pork dishes are the house speciality including stuffed pork – rather strange in a fishing town. But the fish is good. Nice old-fashioned service and imaginative menu. Good carafe wine. Meals L8,000-12,000. Closed Mondays and October-May.

Hotel Primavera, via Pentimele: not quite so good as the excellent

The scenery becomes less inspiring as you move on, but the 'short' cut across the toe of Italy, although with lovely mountain scenery, is almost as long because of zigzags, also slow and extremely hard work for the driver, with bad road surfaces in places.

Though, because of earthquake destruction, it is large and modern, Reggio is surprisingly pleasant. It has views across to Messina in Sicily, a backcloth of the

Excelsior, but rooms much cheaper. Air-conditioning. Meals L7,000-12,000; rooms L19,000-28,000.

For fish, try Restaurant Baylik, vico Leone.

Aspromonte mountains, green with woods, turning white with snow in winter. Tropical plants grow in the surrounding gardens, palms line the Lungomare, the seaside promenade which is flanked by modern buildings and Greek and Roman remains. Reggio was a Greek city, founded in 750 BC, and its museum contains Greek treasures. It has a 15th-century Spanish castle, 17th-century cathedral, and a scientific institute which extracts oil from fruit for perfumes – above all, from the bergamot which is like a small bitter yellow orange. With rose-petal spirit from Bulgaria, it is the most prized perfume ingredient. It grows nowhere else and no one knows where it came from. Its export brings Reggio millions of lire a year. Reggio also makes pipes from huge briar roots found in the mountains. A British consul gave them the idea, possibly by watching Mount Etna smoking across the Straits of Messina. Strangest sight of Reggio is to see the swordfish boats working. They carry an enormous tall

Reggio di
Calabria
continued

steel mast, with a steel
catwalk at right-angles. A
man walks along it to a
platform and spears the
huge fish. You can get a
hydrofoil (15 minutes) or a
car ferry (55 minutes) from
Reggio to Messina in Sicily.

S18 to
Scilla (23 km),
Palmi (26 km),
Rosarno (19 km),
then local roads
left through
Nicotera to
Tropea (about
120 km from
Reggio)

Scilla – La Sirène: on the
beach; good fresh fish;
seven rooms; cheap.

At Scilla stands the granite
crag of Homer's *Odyssey*
where there lived the
monster with seven heads
who terrified sailors.
Opposite is Charybdis with
treacherous currents which
even frightened the
Argonauts. Now that ships
have improved, it is just a
place of superb views
across to Sicily, the Aeolian
Isles of Lipari and volcanic
Stromboli. Scilla has a little
walled harbour at the foot
of the crag and the remains
of a castle built around
300 BC and improved by the
Normans capping it. The
best view is from piazza
Alta.

Palmi	Many good inexpensive fish restaurants – try La Lampara, lido Tonnara: good swordfish. La Marinella, Marinella cove: special pasta, sheep's milk cheese (pecorino), and fine fish.	Palmi is a modern beach resort.
Tropea	Hotel La Pineta: quiet, in orange grove 100 metres from beach. Open May-October; restaurant open only June-September. Meals L8,000-12,000; rooms L20,000-30,000. Virgilio, in village: meals L7,000-11,000; rooms with WC and shower reasonably priced, L16,000-26,000.	Tropea is delightful – a fishing port built into a cliff with a beach of fine white sand and views across to the Aeolian Isles. My favourite Calabrian seaside town. A new resort built alongside the town has not yet spoiled it.
S322 to Pizzo (31 km) then S18 to St Eufemia Lamezia (airport for shorter fly-drive route) (26 km), Paola (61 km) to Cetraro (20 km)	Cetraro: Hotel San Michele: nice restful hotel 5 km north on S18 high above sea; lift to private pebbly beach. Excellent service; pleasant rooms. Meals L12,500; rooms L23,000-35,000. Open April-October.	Paola – see route down from Naples. Cetraro – another little resort, not mentioned on downward journey, but useful for an overnight because of its pleasant hotel.
S18 to Maratea and Sapri (84 km)	Maratea has the Hotel Santavenere: one of Italy's finest, but you may only be able to get in half-*pensione* and it is very dear. A meal	Maratea, on a mountain slope running down to the sea; resort. The higher village has lovely views over the bay, especially at

Maratea
continued

would cost at least
L20,000, probably
L25,000.

Villa Flora: nearer my price
range. Open June–
September. Meals L8,000–
10,000; eight rooms
L16,800.

San Biaglo, 4 km upwards.
Picturesque port.

Sapri is an old-fashioned
seaside resort;
unpretentious.

S104, then
S585 to join
motorway A3
to Salerno
(166 km)

From Salerno, if time is short, you can get the
motorway to Naples airport (56 km). If not, take
the beautiful Amalfi drive, which is hard work for
the driver but gives the passengers wonderful
scenic views. Do not be afraid to hoot loudly on
corners.

Amalfi drive passes the little resorts of Maiori,
Minori, Ravello, Atrani, Amalfi, some reached by
tiny roads steep down to the sea and all charming.
Then Positano, with crowded steep narrow streets,
Sorrento, Vico Equense (with Marina di Equa, with
the splendid Axidie Hotel off to the left just as you
enter).

For all these resorts, see Fly-drive Naples route.
Rejoin Naples motorway at Castellamare di Stabia.
S163 to Sorrento, S145 to Castellamare, A3 to
Naples.
Salerno to Sorrento 68 km,
Sorrento to Castellamare 19 km,
Castellamare to Naples 29 km.

Index

Foods, wines, etc. are printed in *italics*. Main descriptive sections on towns and places of interest are shown in **bold** figures

Arthur Eperon
Travellers' France £2.50

Six major routes across France, taking in the best restaurants and
hotels, visiting the most interesting out-of-the-way places. This
detailed and up-to-the-minute handbook is for the traveller who
wants more out of France than a mad dash down the motorway. Each
of the six routes across the country is illustrated with a specially
commissioned two-colour map, and includes a host of information on
where to eat and drink, where to take children, where to stay, and
how to get the most out of the towns and countryside.

Pan Languages
Travellers' French   Travellers' Dutch
Travellers' German   Travellers' Greek
Travellers' Italian   Travellers' Portuguese
Travellers' Spanish   Travellers' Serbo-Croat
                        for Yugoslavia

A new series of *modern* phrase books developed from the
results of a nationwide Gallup survey of the needs of modern
travellers abroad. They will prove invaluable companions in any
holiday or business situation.

Special features include
. outstandingly clear and easy-to-use design
. specially prepared, simplified pronunciation
. helpful background information
. 'likely answers' sections
. unique section to help practise basic phrases

plus index, conversion tables, map, reference section.

Publication spring and summer 1981.

John Slater
Just Off the Motorway £1.95

The new and enlarged edition of a sensational bestseller.
Introduction by Russell Harty.

Here's the new, bang-up-to-date edition of the handbook everyone
needs. Detailed research, careful sampling, and more than 150 maps
show where you can find any service you require – cheaper and
better – by turning off at a junction and driving no more than
three miles off the motorway – eating, drinking, overnight stops,
breakdown services, petrol, visits.

'Worth a detour to buy it' DAILY MAIL

George Morrison
An Irish Camera £1.75

Ireland a century ago – as it was recorded by the pioneers
of photography. The streets of Dublin and Belfast, the green
countryside and the grim industries, traditional village life, all the
charmed atmosphere and social reality of Victorian Ireland.
Introduction by Harold Clarke.

'Sixty-four of the earliest photographs ... carefully chosen ... must
be the best value for money yet in its field' IRISH WEEKLY

Francis Hitching
The World Atlas of Mysteries £5.50

From the origins of the universe and terrestrial life, through the unique
development of man, to the secrets of ancient civilizations and bizarre
phenomena in the sky and beyond – the enormous scope of this
encyclopedia, its exhaustive research and copious illustrations
(maps, photographs, diagrams) make it a unique and fascinating
book. Francis Hitching, author of *Earth Magic*, is one of the world's
leading authorities on the inexplicable and the unexplained.

compiled by Jonathon Green
Famous Last Words £1.50

'They couldn't hit an elephant at this distance—' last words of an American general ... Deathbed wisdom, gallows humour, suicide notes, fond farewells, desperate departures – here is a fascinating anthology of exit lines, over two thousand entries featuring the world's leading figures: Lincoln, Oscar Wilde, Bing Crosby, Julius Caesar, Henry VIII, Noel Coward, Hitler, Van Gogh, Billy the Kid.

'Compulsively entertaining' SUNDAY EXPRESS

Andrew Barrow
Gossip 1920–1970 £3.95

The twenties had their Bright Young Things, the sixties their pop aristocracy. The columnists of the five decades 1920–70 were never at a loss to reveal the scandals of elopements, parties, sex changes, court cases and the rest. Drawn from newspapers, diaries and biographies, this book is a fascinating chronicle of the Rolls-Royce, diamond-tiara, private-plane, chilled-champagne set.

'Juicy little snippets ... the only reasonable excuse for breaking the silence over the breakfast table' SUNDAY TELEGRAPH

Robert Morley
Robert Morley's Book of Worries £1.50

Do you have sleepless nights worrying about money, sex, age, diet, cars – even being buried alive or having an aeroplane fall on you? You do? Then take heart, for there is at least one other person like you – Robert Morley to be exact.

Increase your anxiety potential with this hilarious guide to worrying peppered with that magic only the master himself can produce.

Bestselling Fiction and Non-Fiction

☐	**Modesty Blaise**	Peter O'Donnell	95p
☐	**Falconhurst Fancy**	Kyle Onstott	£1.50p
☐	**The Pan Book of Card Games**	Hubert Phillips	£1.25p
☐	**The New Small Garden**	C. E. Lucas Phillips	£2.50p
☐	**Fools Die**	Mario Puzo	£1.50p
☐	**Everything Your Doctor Would Tell You If He Had the Time**	Claire Rayner	£4.95p
☐	**Polonaise**	Piers Paul Read	95p
☐	**The 65th Tape**	Frank Ross	£1.25p
☐	**Nightwork**	Irwin Shaw	£1.25p
☐	**Bloodline**	Sidney Sheldon	95p
☐	**A Town Like Alice**	Nevil Shute	£1.25p
☐	**Lifeboat VC**	Ian Skidmore	£1.00p
☐	**Just Off the Motorway**	John Slater	£1.95p
☐	**Wild Justice**	Wilbur Smith	£1.50p
☐	**The Spoiled Earth**	Jessica Stirling	£1.75p
☐	**That Old Gang of Mine**	Leslie Thomas	£1.25p
☐	**Caldo Largo**	Earl Thompson	£1.50p
☐	**Future Shock**	Alvin Toffler	£1.95p
☐	**The Visual Dictionary of Sex**	Eric J. Trimmer	£5.95p
☐	**The Flier's Handbook**		£4.95p

All these books are available at your local bookshop or newsagent, or
can be ordered direct from the publisher. Indicate the number of copies
required and fill in the form below

. . . .

Name _____
(block letters please)

Address _____

_____

Send to Pan Books (CS Department), Cavaye Place, London SW10 9PG
Please enclose remittance to the value of the cover price plus:

25p for the first book plus 10p per copy for each additional book ordered
to a maximum charge of £1.05 to cover postage and packing
Applicable only in the UK

While every effort is made to keep prices low, it is sometimes
necessary to increase prices at short notice. Pan Books reserve
the right to show on covers and charge new retail prices which
may differ from those advertised in the text or elsewhere